The Art of
CARICATURING

The Art of
CARICATURING

A Series of Lessons Covering

All Branches of the Art of Caricaturing

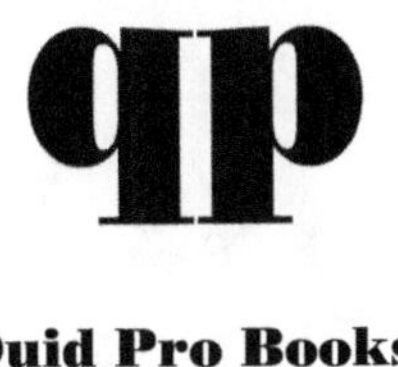

Quid Pro Books

New Orleans, Louisiana

Originally published in 1941 by Frederick J. Drake & Co., Publishers, Chicago; and copyright © 1941 by Frederick J. Drake & Co. No copyright is claimed in the original text and illustrations.

Published in 2012 by Quid Pro Books. A *Digitally Remastered Book*.™

ISBN 978-1-61027-913-0 (pbk)

QUID PRO BOOKS
Quid Pro, LLC
5860 Citrus Blvd., Suite D-101
New Orleans, Louisiana 70123
www.quidprobooks.com

The Art of
CARICATURING

The Art of CARICATURING

A Series of Lessons Covering All Branches of the Art of Caricaturing

BY

Mitchell Smith

FULLY ILLUSTRATED

•

CHICAGO

FREDERICK J. DRAKE & CO.

Publishers

Foreword

In the writing and illustrating of this book my aim has been to produce a comprehensive and concise treatise on the art of caricaturing. It has been made as brief as is consistent with clearness and completeness.

Although the text is brief, no illustrations were spared. The many plates illustrate all points necessary, and each of the points illustrated are explained in the text with reference to that particular illustration. In addition to the plates there are many caricatures of famous men included.

Acting upon the assumption that it is easier to work if ones assignments are already made, Chapter XII has been made up of assignments and suggestions, which makes this book a complete course in caricaturing.

If you obtain half as much pleasure and profit from the use of this book as I derived from writing, and especially illustrating it, I shall consider my time well spent.

Wishing you much success.

Mitchell Smith.

Contents

List of Illustrations

PEN and INK LINES

A
DRAWN WITH GIL-
LOTTS PEN #303

B
MAKE LIGHT TONES
WITH FINE LINES,

C
OR WIDELY SPACED
LINES. C AND D

D
ARE CALLED SHAKY
OR IRREGULAR LINES

E
E, F AND G ARE

F
CROSSHATCH LINES

G
C AND D COMBINED

H
HERRINGBONE WEAVE

I
HEAVY LINES, OR

J
CLOSELY SPACED,

K
OR SOLID BLACK

L
FOR DARK AREAS

M
SPATTER WORK

N
DOTS WITH BRUSH

O
GRADED

P
GRADED

Q
DECREASED PRESSURE

R
INCREASED

S
T
U

V
W
STAMPED WITH CLOTH AND KNIT PADS

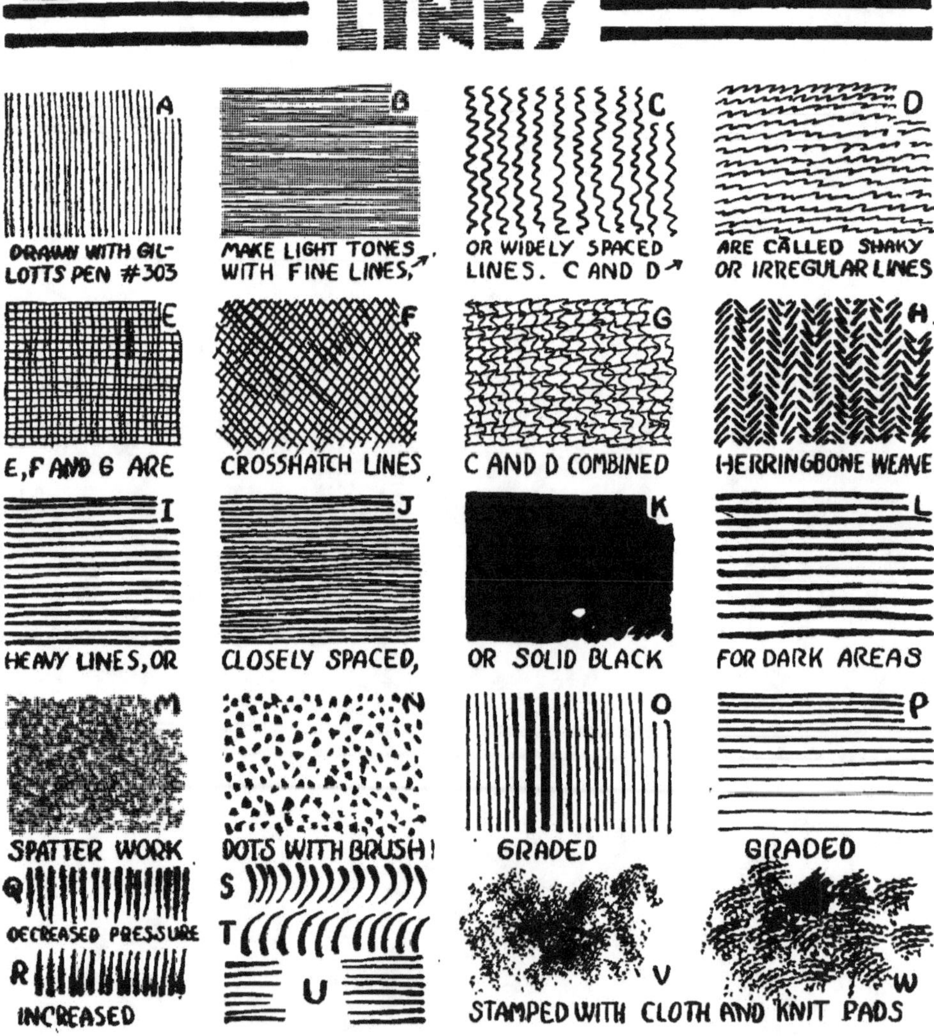

PLATE 1

Chapter I

Pen Lines and Materials

The necessary material used in drawing caricatures are few and inexpensive if we compare them to the tools of some of the professions, such as surgery, etc.

The student of caricaturing should procure a number of drawing pens in various sizes. Gillotts drawing pens are perhaps the most widely used of all pens by cartoonists and pen and ink artists in general. For drawing cartoons and caricatures sizes 170, 303 and 404 are the ones most used. Other sizes and styles of pens may be very useful; especially bowl point pens for drawing heavy lines for the outlines of cartoons. In this book are reproduced a number of caricatures that were outlined with a lettering pen which enabled the artist to get an effect markedly original. These lettering pens may be had in many sizes, and shaped with round, square or oblong nibs. The student, or, prospective student is advised to obtain some of these, because every artist should learn to manipulate the lettering pen and brush in lettering. Nearly all art work requires more or less hand lettering.

Other materials needed are, black waterproof drawing ink—Higgins is very good—and pencils for sketching and drawing. All drawings should be completely drawn with pencil before drawing in ink. Art gum erasers, thumb tacks for fastening the drawing paper or board to the drawing board will also be needed. The most satisfactory material to make the drawings on is a good grade of Bristol Board. But if the drawings are not intended for publication, a good quality of heavy, hard surface bond paper gives satisfactory results, and is also very good for sketching. Caricaturing requires a great deal of sketching, and one should keep a supply of good paper for this purpose, to record ideas and impressions before they escape from the mind never to return from that oblivion where all things mental and material eventually go.

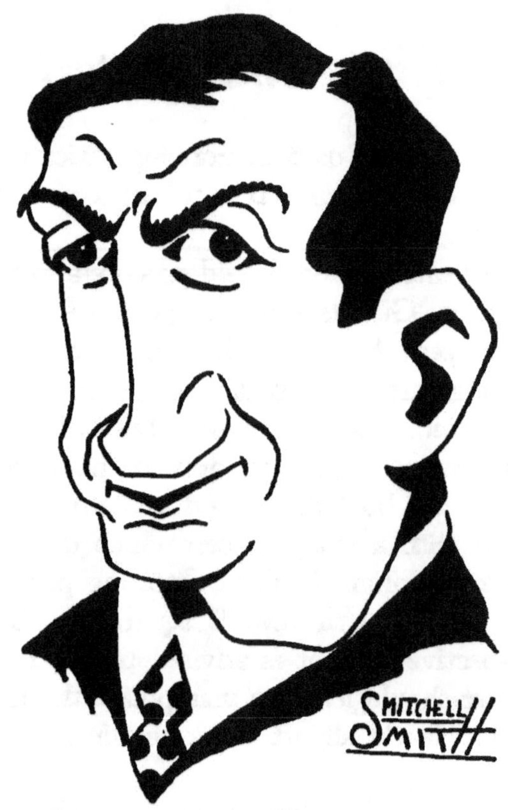

NICOLA

After which sudden outburst of scholarship and philosophy, let us consider the manipulation of the pen, for the benefit of beginners who are not familiar with this medium of drawing.

The drawing pen is held the same as in the proper position for writing; that is, with the thumb and first and second fingers of the right hand.

A variety of pen lines are used in cartooning and caricaturing. Fine lines, heavy lines, slow lines, fast lines, irregular lines, and shaky

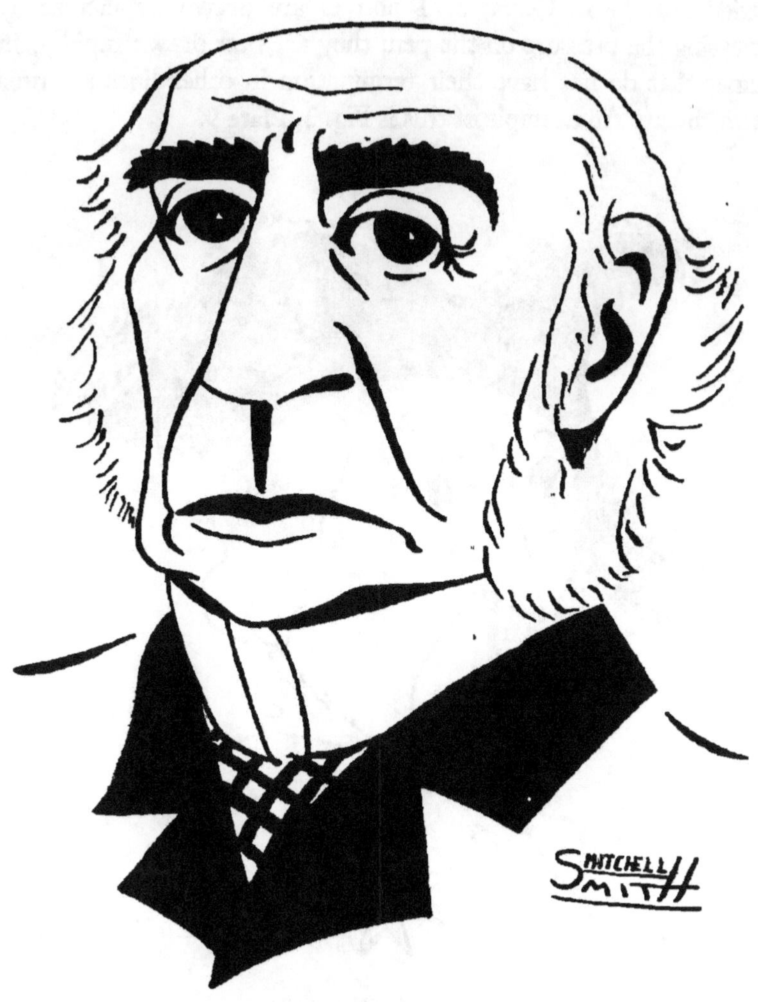

GLADSTONE

lines are most frequently used. On **Plate 1** are illustrations of various kinds of lines, dots, shading and etc. E, F and G are called **crosshatch** lines and they are used for **shading**. There are some examples of crosshatch in the illustrations in this book; especially, of **F, Plate 1.**

Graded lines as in Q, R, S, T and U are drawn by increasing or decreasing the pressure on the pen; they are best drawn rapidly. Ends of lines that do not have their termination in other lines are usually drawn thusly. An example of this is Fig. 3, **Plate 9**.

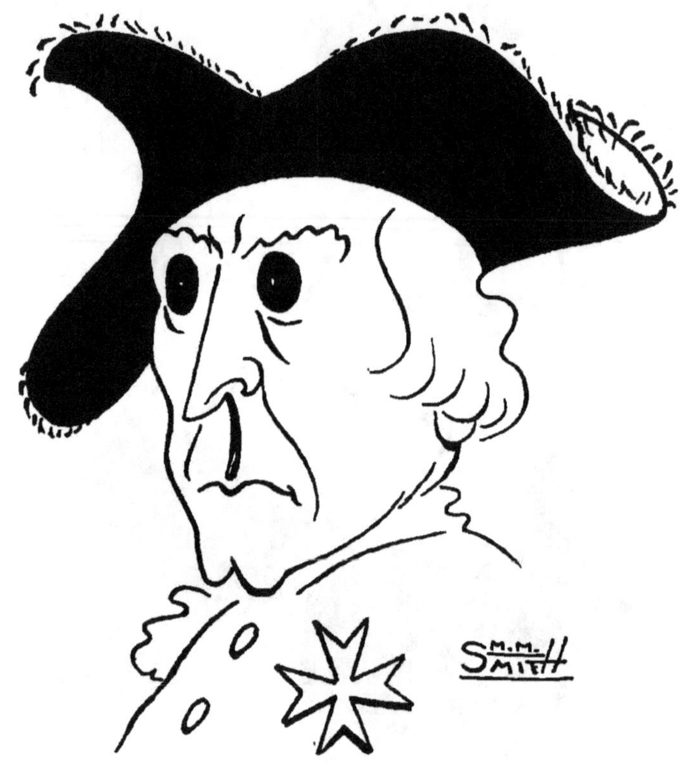

FREDERICK THE GREAT

K on **Plate 1** was made with a small camels hair brush, which every cartoonist should have. L is also drawn with the same brush. Lines such as these are sometimes used to stripe trousers. See Fig. 4, **Plate 10**. N is dots drawn with the brush, and M is termed **Spatter**, which will be explained later.

V and W are stamped with pads of denim and knit goods, respectively. One can often create something original by experimenting, and trying many ways and techniques of drawing an object, or caricature. The same pad used in stamping W was used in drawing the caricature of Robert Herrick.

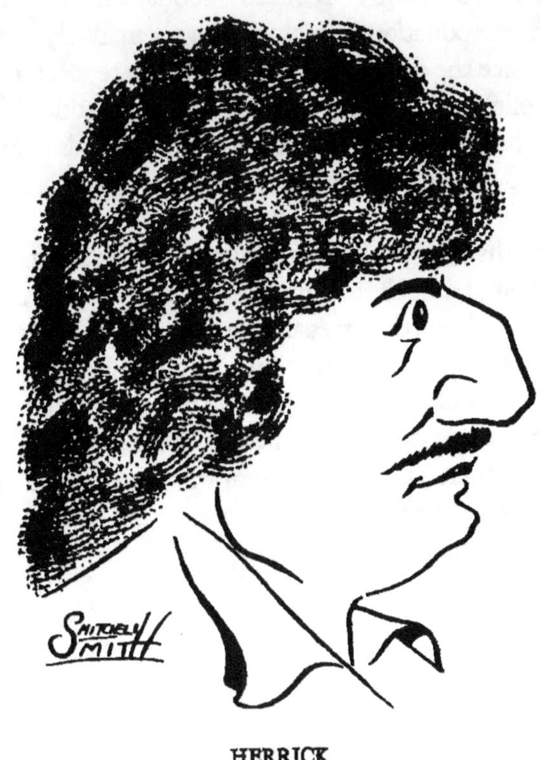

HERRICK

In the drawing of caricatures and cartoons—or any other commercial art, for that matter—the artist should know something about the processes of reproduction for that particular form of art work. For pen and ink work the engraving is made on a zinc printing plate. It is not necessary, however, to know all about these processes of reproduction. The artist should know that all work intended for line reproductions should be made on white paper or Bristol Board with black drawing ink. The drawing to be reproduced is photographed on a chemically treated zinc plate, which is then treated with acid. This acid eats away the surface of the zinc, except the photographed lines, which are left in relief, somewhat like printing type. Colored inks do not photograph well; neither does black ink on colored paper.

Drawings are usually reduced about one-half the original dimensions in reproduction, which makes them really one-fourth the original size. Since the dimensions are, of course, reduced in proportion, it naturally follows that the pen lines are also reduced in the same proportion in breadth, or thickness. Therefore, in drawing for reproduction one should use heavier lines than appear in a printed drawing.

Study the many drawings in this book to see how they have been drawn. Notice that the outlines are invariably the heaviest, while the lines for shading and such, are finer. Notice also how the lines have been drawn, and how the pressure on the pen has been decreased gradually at the end of lines to taper them, and avoid that **cut off** appearance that results from bringing the pen to an abrupt stop at the same pressure, making the entire line the same thickness.

Study an accomplished artist's work and take advantage of what he knows, and put your own original ideas in the drawing. This is the road that leads to success in art.

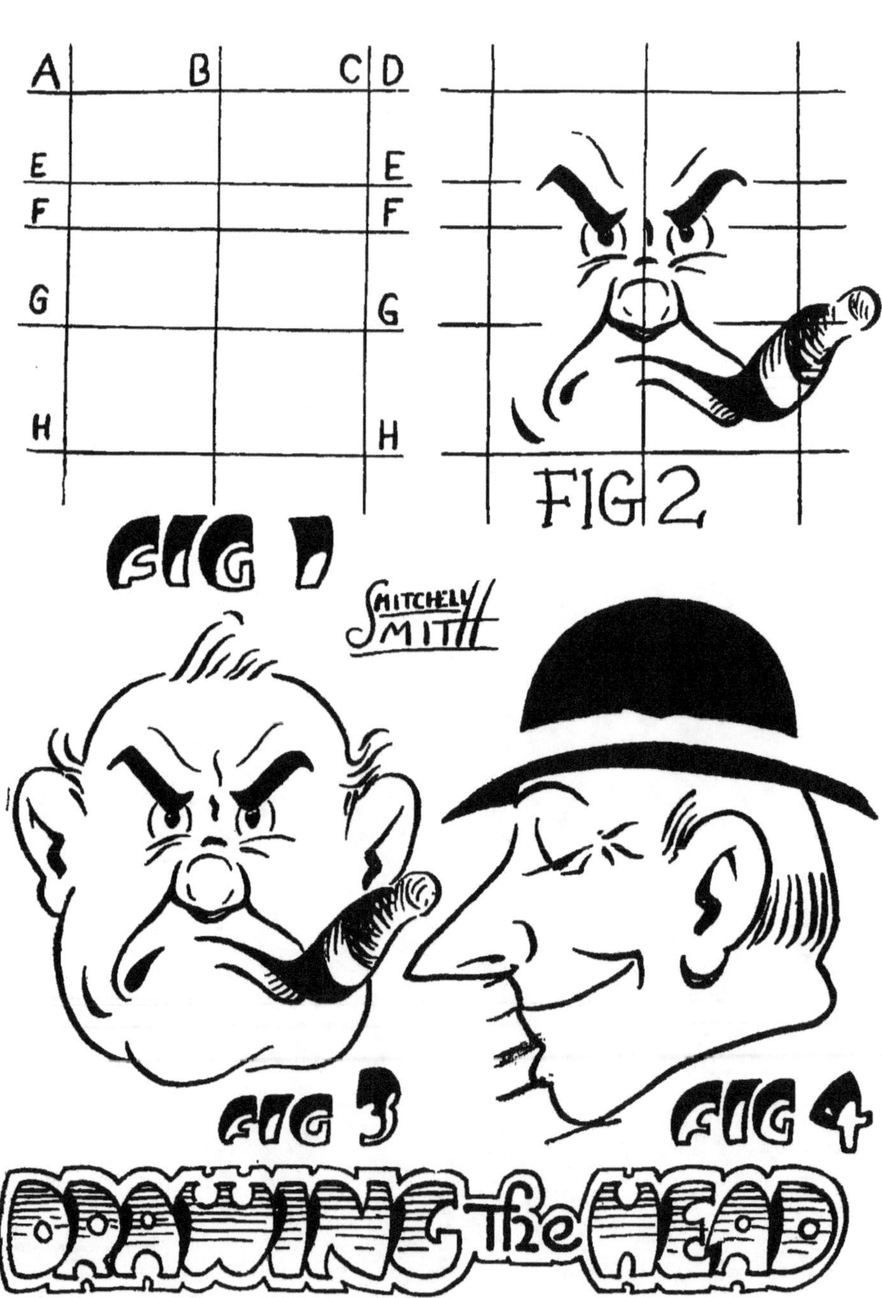
A B C D
E E
F F
G G
H H
FIG 1
FIG 2
MITCHELL SMITH
FIG 3
FIG 4
DRAWING The HEAD

Chapter II

The Face and Head

The head is not so difficult to learn to draw, but to learn to draw it well requires diligent study and practice. It may not seem reasonable to the beginner when told that it is much easier to learn to draw the head well, than it is to draw hands well.

Although the features of the head and face are exaggerated in cartoons, in life they follow closely definite proportions. These proportions are as follows: The eyes are about midway between the top of the head and the bottom of the chin; the nose is as long as the distance from the nose to the bottom of the chin, and the mouth is one third of the distance from the end of the nose to the bottom of the chin; the top of the ears are about on a line with the eyebrows, and the bottoms on a line with the end of the nose.

To draw a front view cartoon of the head, draw a perpendicular line for the center of the face, as B, Fig. 1, Plate 2. This line will be equidistant from the eyes and split the nose and mouth in two equal parts. Near the center of this line draw a horizontal line, as FF, Fig. 1. Next draw line EE for the brows and the top of the ears, and GG as a guide for the bottom of the ears and end of nose. Lines A and C, Fig. 1 are drawn equidistant from, and parallel to, line B. These are all the lines necessary in drawing a cartoon, but in drawing a caricature of a definite face it is better to make guide lines for the top of the head and bottom of chin in the proportions outlined in the preceding paragraph. The next step is to place the features with a pencil, beginning with the eyes; brows, second; nose, third; mouth, fourth; ears, fifth; and finish by drawing hair, chin, etc.

There are many ways of drawing the features in a cartoon, which vary with the different expressions. Since the subject of this book is

23

AS CROWN PRINCE
FIG 4
MITCHELL SMITH
FIG 1
FIG 2
DRAWN FROM LATE PHOTO
FIG 3
EX-KAISER
WILLIAM II
FIG 5

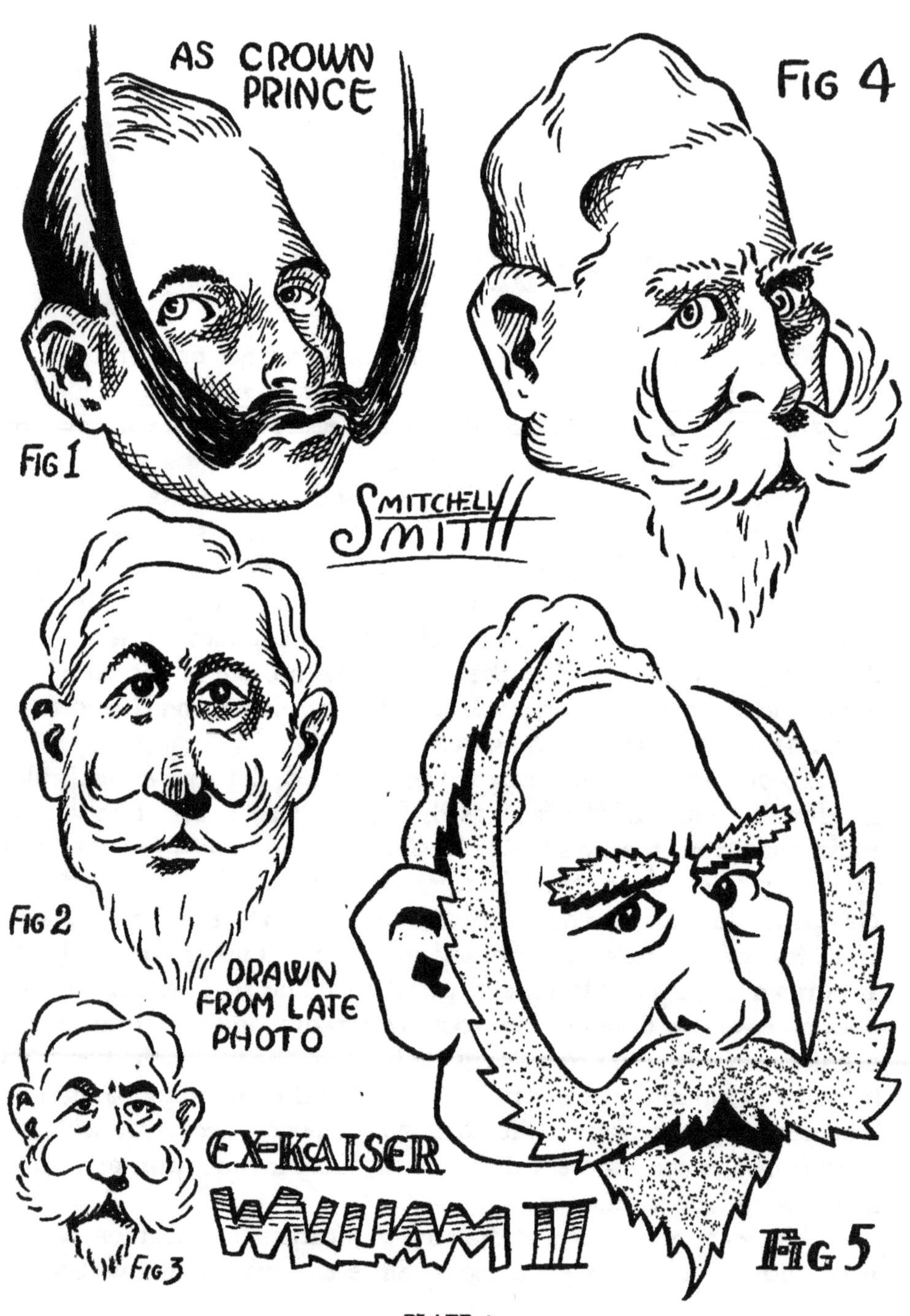

PLATE 3

caricaturing, only this will be dealt with here. The features are drawn lifelike in caricatures, except in ones where extreme exaggeration is used. To make a drawing appear lifelike is rather difficult for beginners, because there are a great many little tricks for doing this, which they do not understand. Some of these methods are illustrated in the caricatures of Von Hindenburg on **Plate 7.** Figure 1 was drawn from a photograph with little exaggeration, while Fig. 2 is exaggerated a great deal. Note in Fig. 2 the outlines for the black shadows under eyebrows, corners of eyes, wrinkles, under nose, under mustache, and under chin on the white collar. These outlined shadows have been blacked in on the large drawing giving it life and sparkle. Attention is called to the highlights on the eyes, also. This is very useful, and is invariably used to make the eyes lifelike. The black bow tie and other shading give the drawing tone, or color, which heightens the effect. Do not forget shadows under ears in profiles, and faces other than directly front views.

Caricatures are either drawn from life, or from photographs or portraits. For the student who has not studied drawing from life it will, perhaps, be easier to get a good likeness by drawing from photographs. In good photographs the wrinkles, shadows, and conspicuous features are more easily seen which helps one to know what to exaggerate to get a good likeness of the subject being caricatured. Highlights on eyes and hair are more easily seen and placed correctly on the drawing. Another advantage of drawing from photographs is that the head is more easily proportioned correctly. This is because the various features can be measured on the photograph and enlarged proportionately in the drawing. For example, if one is going to make the drawing five times as high as the head in the photograph, he can determine the correct proportions because he can measure the width of the head on the photo and get the width of the head in the drawing accordingly. The nose, mouth and other features may likewise be measured and placed correctly.

However, one disadvantage of drawing from photographs is that you can only get one view to work from, unless you have photographs in different positions of the same subject. With two positions it is sometimes possible to construct a third view. How this is done is illustrated on **Plate 3** with the caricatures of Ex-Kaiser William. Figure

1 on this plate was drawn from an old photo taken while he was Crown Prince. Fig. 2 was made from a late photograph. By using these two drawings a third (Fig. 4) was constructed showing the old man with

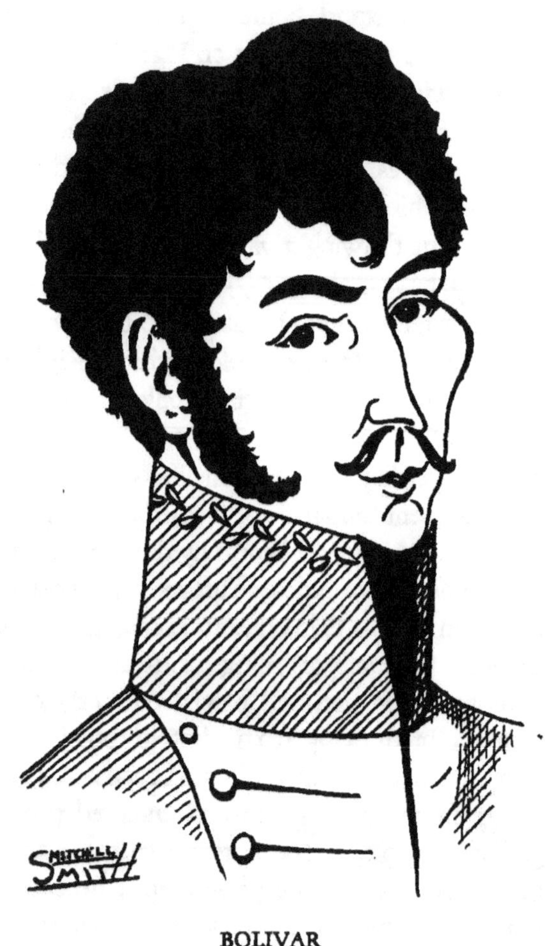

BOLIVAR

the same view as the one as Crown Prince. Figures 3 and 5 are simply caricatures of the same subject in different techniques and degrees of exaggeration. The shape of the nose, forehead, hair, and other features in Figures 4 and 5 are such that it was possible to draw a profile also.

Although drawing from photographs has some advantages,

drawing from life also has its advantages. In life drawing many sketches of different views and positions can be made to determine the best, and this should always be done when possible. Caricatures of some subjects are better drawn in profile, while others are improved by using other positions. There is only one sure way to determine which is best, and that is by experiment.

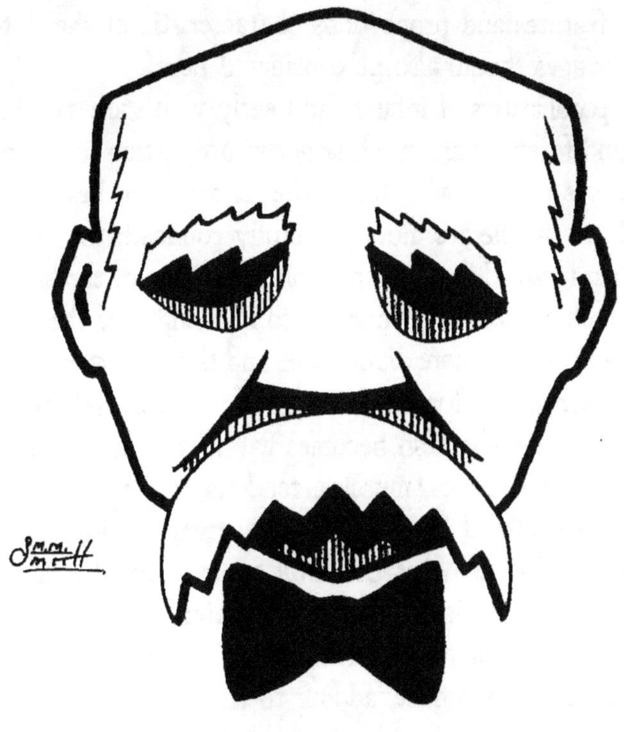

CLEMENCEAU

There is also a way to measure from life to aid the artist in getting the true proportions in making a drawing. To do this, hold a pencil in a vertical position at arms length and sight over the top of pencil, putting the top of pencil in line with the top of the head, or whatever object you are measuring. Next place the thumb on the pencil in line with the bottom of chin. The length of pencil from your thumb to the top, will be used for the height of the head in your drawing, placing guide lines that far apart. The pencil is then held horizontally to determine the width of the drawing. The height of forehead, length of nose, chin, etc., can be properly proportioned by using this method. This method is not only useful in drawing from life, but is good for drawing from still life, also.

The features and proportions characteristic of the difference in the various ages should also be considered here.

The peculiarities of infancy and early youth are as follows: The cranium and forehead are much larger in proportion to the rest of the head; the eyes are somewhat below the center of the head; the features and head as a whole are more gracefully rounded; the neck is much smaller than in an adult, in proportion to the size of the head; and the legs are much shorter in proportion to the length of the torso. With age the head becomes more diminutive, and the bony structure becomes more prominent at the forehead, bridge of the nose, and the jaw bones.

With old age the flesh becomes flabby and falls away from the bones, causing the bones, muscles, tendons, and blood vessels to be more in evidence; and furrowing the face with wrinkles in the face and forehead. The dome of the skull appears broader, and the face shorter, caused by the loss of teeth and straightening of the lower jaw bones. The nose is more powerful if not larger and the features in general are more prominent, adding to the character and dignity of years. The eyes also appear deeper in their sockets, which illusion is caused by the aforementioned relaxation and drooping of the flesh above and below the eyes.

Models of advanced age are easier to draw, and to get a good likeness of, because of these characteristics mentioned in the preceding paragraph. The smooth rounded features of youth are difficult to draw and obtain a good likeness for the reason that there is nothing, or very little at most, in one to distinguish it from another. This is the reason that women and children are seldom good subjects for caricaturing.

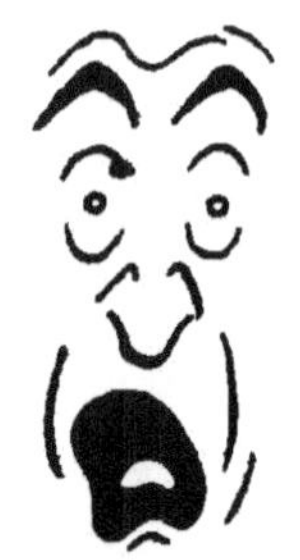

FRIGHT

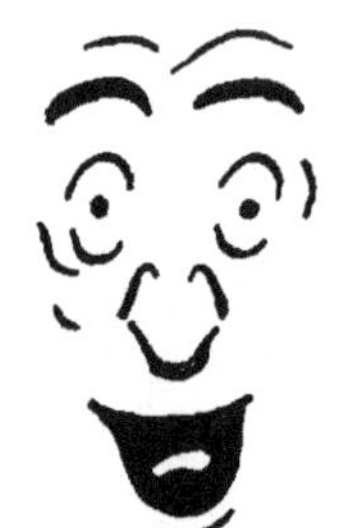

SURPRISE

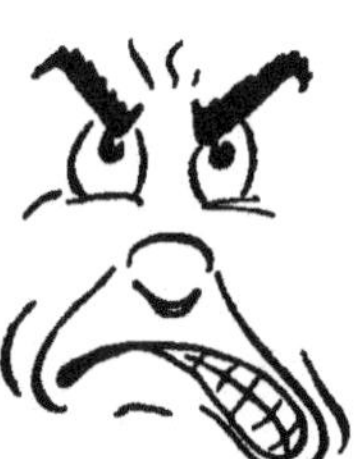

ANGER

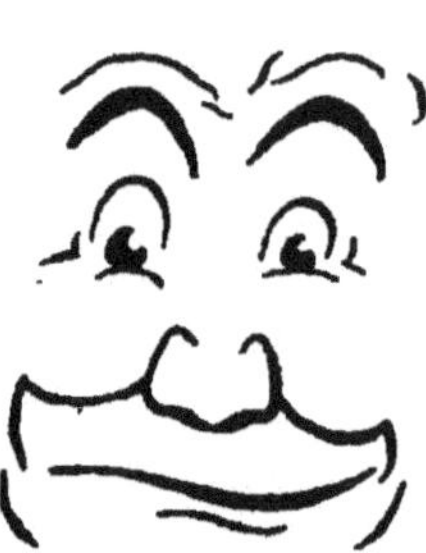

ATTENTION

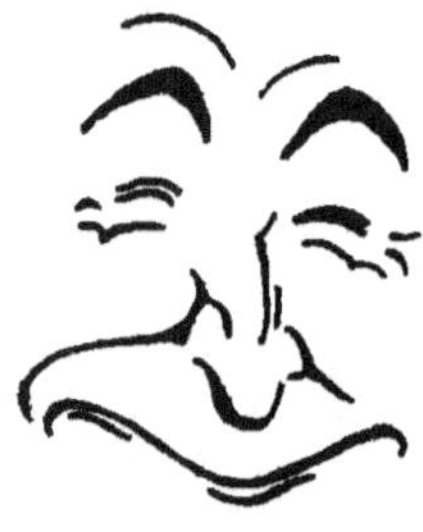

SMILE

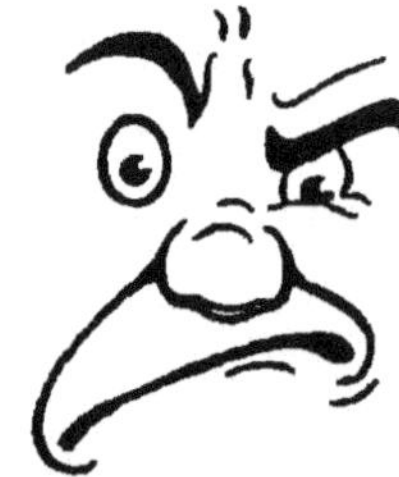

SNEER

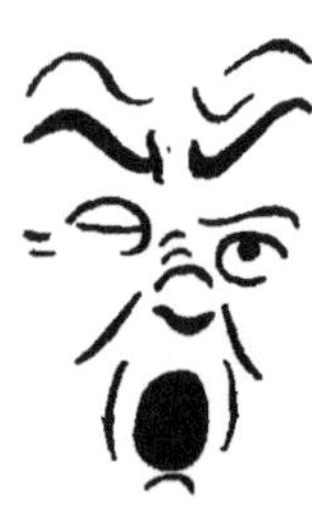

PAIN

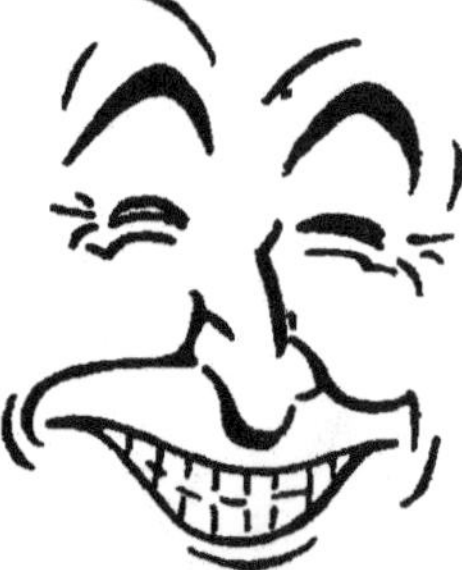

LAUGHTER

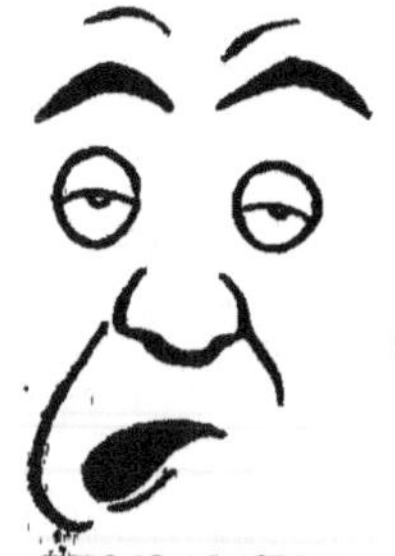

STUPIDITY

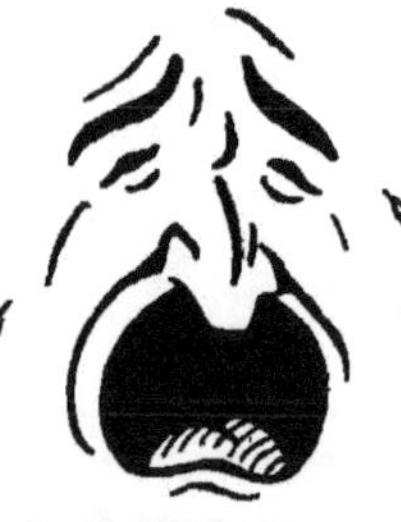

WEEPING

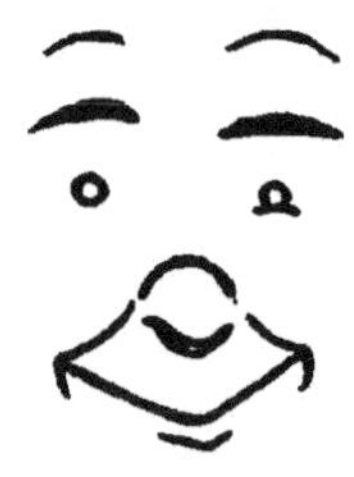

ANTICIPATION

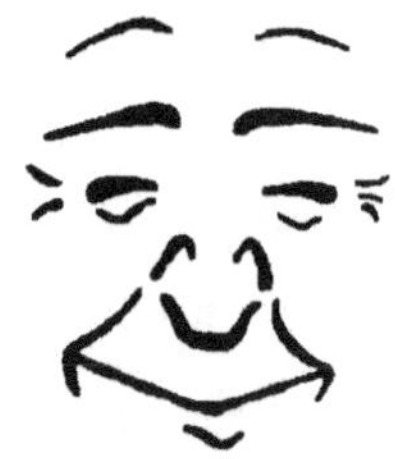

CONTENTMENT

EXPRESSIONS

PLATE 4

Chapter III

Expression

Expression is very important in cartooning and caricaturing. Just as a cartoon is an exaggerated drawing, so is the expression in a cartoon exaggerated.

On **Plate 4** are illustrations of twelve of the most used expressions. They are labeled underneath each drawing: **fright, surprise, anger, attention, smile, sneer, pain, laughter, stupidity, weeping, anticipation, and contentment.** Study these drawings carefully and analyze each expression. To help you do this, each expression shall be considered separately and their main characteristics noted.

In **fright** the eyebrows are lifted and the forehead wrinkled. The eyes are opened very wide, and so is the mouth; and the hair stands on end.

Surprise is similar to fright except that the mouth is not opened as wide and the eyebrows are not lifted as much.

In **Anger** the brows are drawn down in the center and are knotted, or knit, and irregular, with the forehead wrinkled vertically. The eyes are partly covered by the brows. The corners of the mouth are drawn downward, and very often the teeth are visible as in the illustration. Also the hair stands on end or is disorderly.

Note in **Attention** the shape of eyes, eyebrows, nose and mouth. Study the wrinkles around the eyes, mouth, and forehead in all the different expressions illustrated.

In **Smiling** the brows are lifted in an arched position. The eyes are partly closed at the corners. The corners of the mouth are drawn upward and may be opened slightly, or closed depending on the particular expression desired.

FIG 1
FIG 2
FIG 3
ADMIRAL
COONTZ
FIG 4
SMITCHELL SMITH
FIG 5
FIG 7
DER FUEHRER
HITLER
FIG 6
FIG 8
FIG 9
EXPRESSION

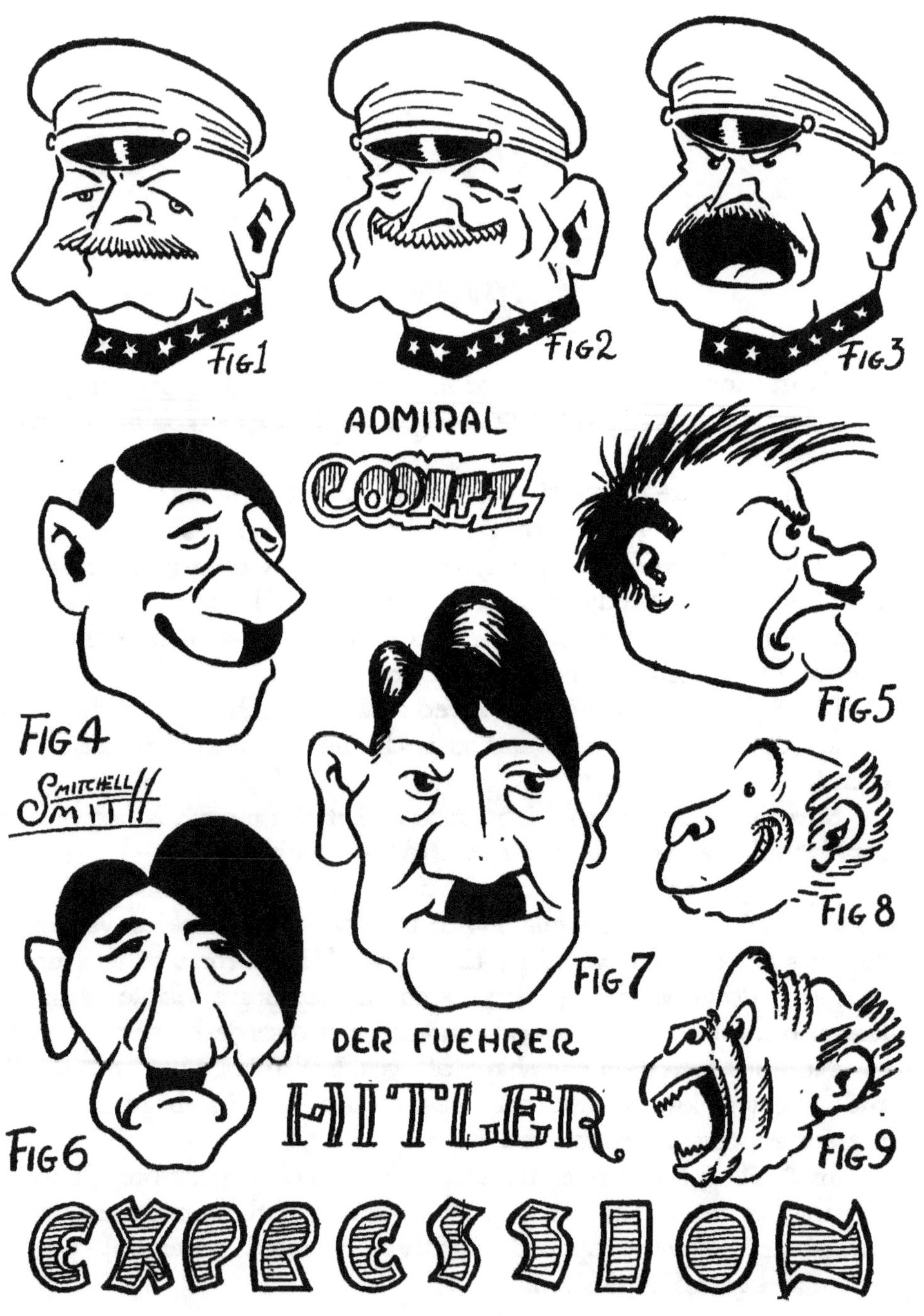

PLATE 5

The expression, **Sneer**, is drawn with one eyebrow drawn down over the eye, which is partly closed. The nose is turned up slightly and wrinkled. One corner of the mouth is up and the other down. The proper relation should be kept between the features. That is, the

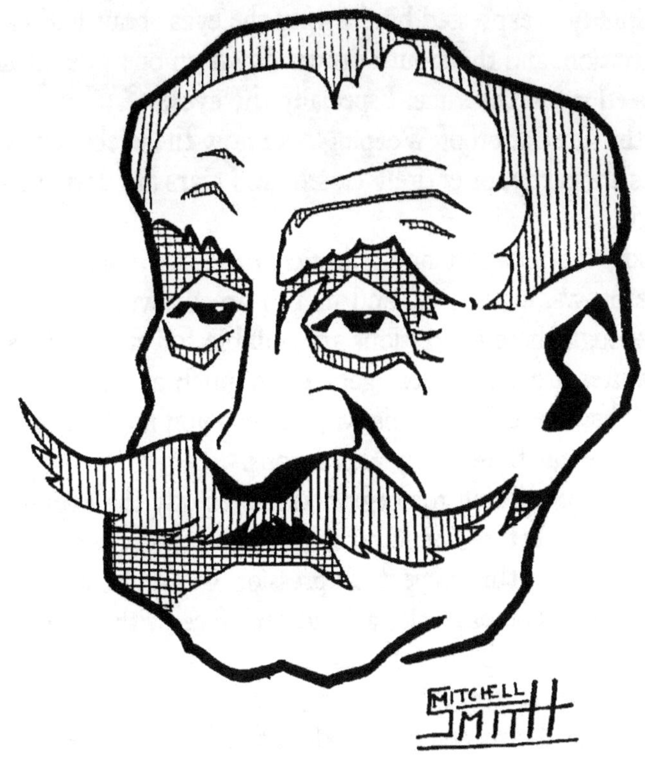

FOCH

corner of the mouth should be elevated on the side on which the eyebrow is down.

The eyebrows in **Pain** are knotted somewhat as in anger. The nose is wrinkled and the mouth is opened. Note particularly the eyes and mouth. Such mouths as are used in the illustrations of fright and surprise would not be suitable here.

Laughter is very similar to smiling. The only difference being, the brows are higher, the eyes more closed, and the mouth opened wider. In **Uproarious Laughter** the nose moves upward to make room for the mouth to stretch big and wide, showing teeth, tongue, tonsils, or what you will.

Stupidity is expressed by drawing the eyes about half closed as in the illustration, and the mouth drawn down on one side. **Drunkenness** is expressed much the same. Especially the eyes.

In the illustration of **Weeping** note how the eyebrows are drawn. The eyes are partly, or entirely closed, and tears are drawn to help the expression.

Study the illustrations of **Anticipation** and **Contentment.** Note how the brows, eyes, nose, and mouth are drawn.

Although these expressions are suitable for cartoons, expressions in caricatures are seldom exaggerated as much as the illustrations on **Plate 4.** They were drawn this way so that you might more easily see how to represent these many expressions.

A very good thing for beginners is to study the expressions used in some of the better comic strips. Popeye, and Moon Mullins are especially good in this respect. Expression should be suited to action and vice versa. For example, a head and face with an expression of fright should have a body with the characteristic action of fright; that is, fingers far apart, feet off the ground, etc.

On **Plate 5** are some reproductions of caricatures in various expressions and poses of some rather famous men: Adolph Hitler and Admiral Coontz. Figure 1 has a stern look obtained by representing the mouth, or really the mustache, in a straight line. In Figures 2 and 3 note that the same general principles were used as in the expressions, "Smile" and "Anger" on **Plate 4.** Figure 4 is a two thirds front view caricature of Hitler, smiling. Figure 5 is a profile of Hitler, angry. His nose trouble (mustache) takes on a new aspect in this drawing; that of a rather stiff brush perhaps. In Fig. 6 he has a grouch, while in Fig. 7 he is rather calm. Figures 8 and 9 are to illustrate that animals can be drawn with almost any expression. However, expression is more difficult with some animals than with others.

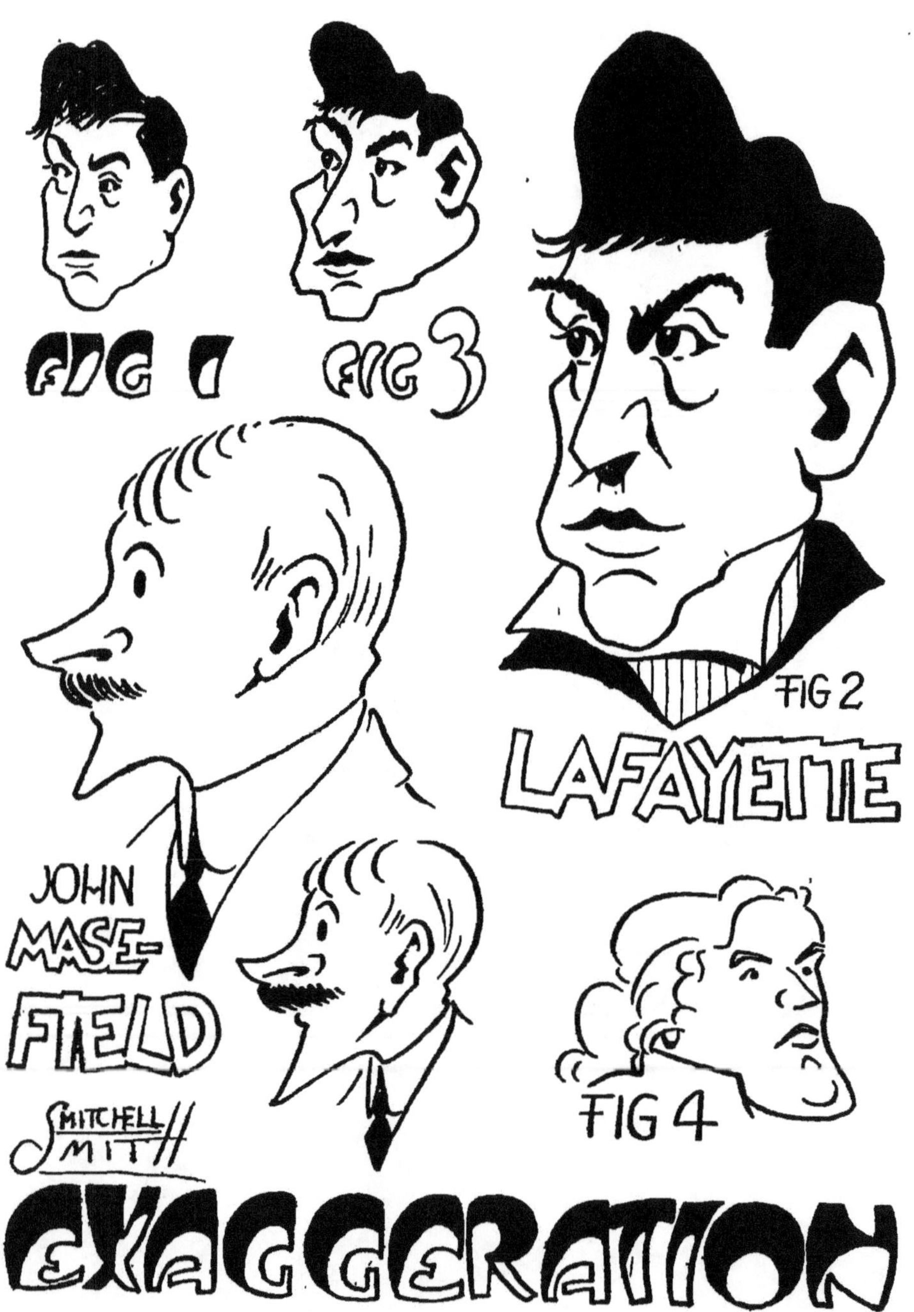
FIG 1
FIG 3
FIG 2
LAFAYETTE
JOHN MASE-FIELD
MITCHELL SMITH
FIG 4
EXAGGERATION

Chapter IV

Exaggeration

Exaggeration is the life of a cartoon or caricature. Really that is what they are—exaggerations. The three forms of exaggeration in a humorous drawing are, exaggeration of form, expression, and action. However, exaggeration of the face and head in caricaturing is the purpose of this chapter, and exaggeration of action will be treated in a separate chapter on action.

A caricature is an exaggerated drawing, having a likeness of one particular person. This statement raises the question of **what** to exaggerate. What to exaggerate depends entirely upon the features of the subject being caricatured. The most noticeable, or prominent features of the model are usually, if not always, accentuated. For example, if the model has a round face and large eyes exaggerate these. See the caricature of Andrew Carnegie on **Plate 14.** If the nose or ears are large exaggerate these as in the caricature on the jacket of this book. Or a prominent jaw may be accentuated as the artist has done in the drawing of Bismarck, Page 39, and Ex-Kaiser Wilhelm II, **Plate 3.** The chin, beard, hair, etc., may also be exaggerated.

Since the caricature is supposed to have a likeness of the carica-tured, it naturally follows that if the most noticeable features are exaggerated, it will be easier to get a likeness of the model. As to the degree of exaggeration, there is only one way to determine what degree will give the best results and resemblance to the model, and that is by experiment. It is always wise to make a number of pencil sketches trying various degrees of exaggeration, and different techniques, before making a finished drawing with pen and ink.

On the Exaggeration **Plate 6,** note the various degrees of exaggeration, used in the drawings of Lafayette, Figures 1, 2, and 3.

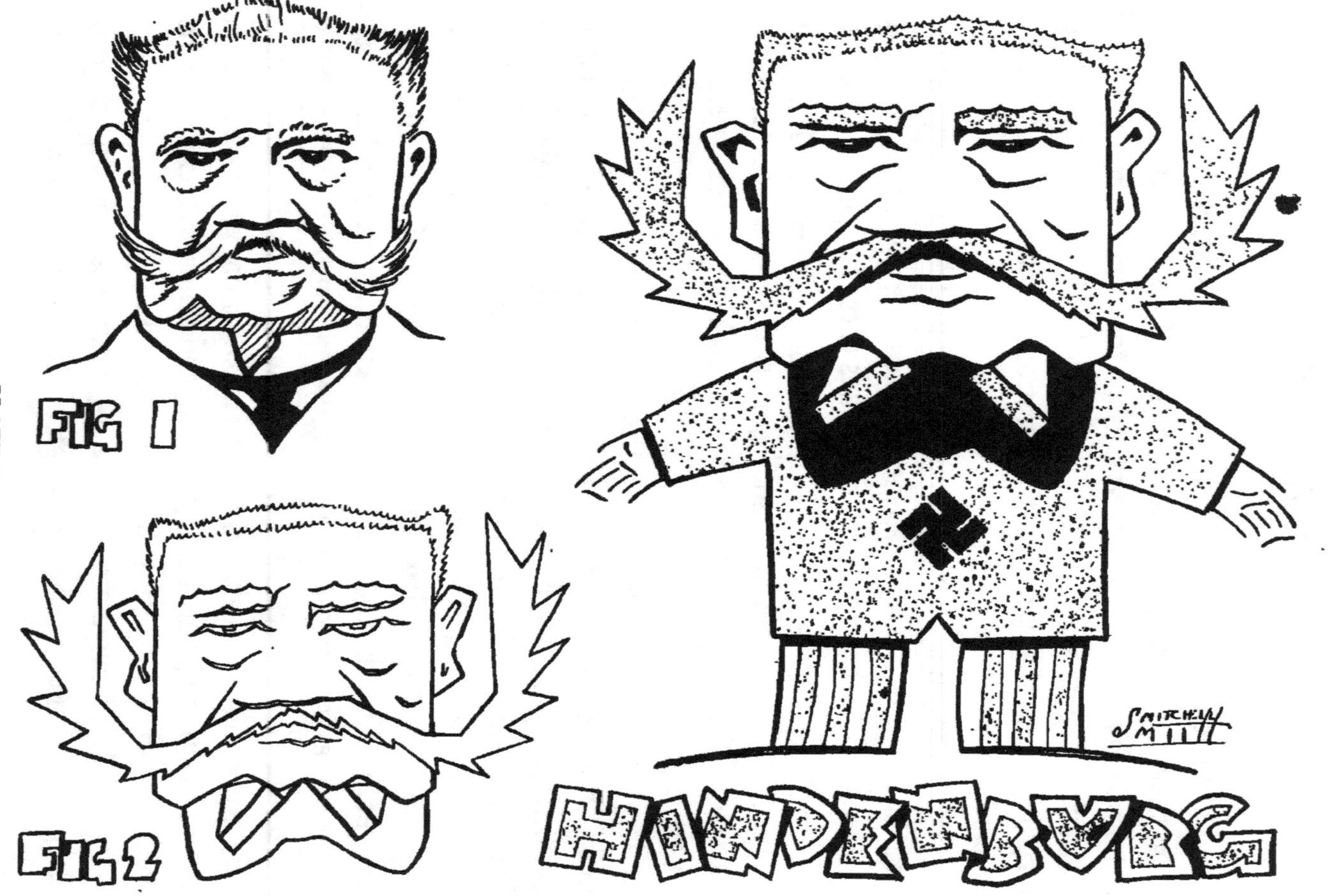

PLATE 7

There is little accentuation in Figure 1, while Figure 2 is exaggerated more, especially the eyes, chin, jaw, and ear. The same features are enlarged in Figure 3, only more so. Figures 1 and 3 are only sketches, and as Figure 2 seemed best, it was made the large finished drawing. Practically the same thing was done in the two drawings of the English

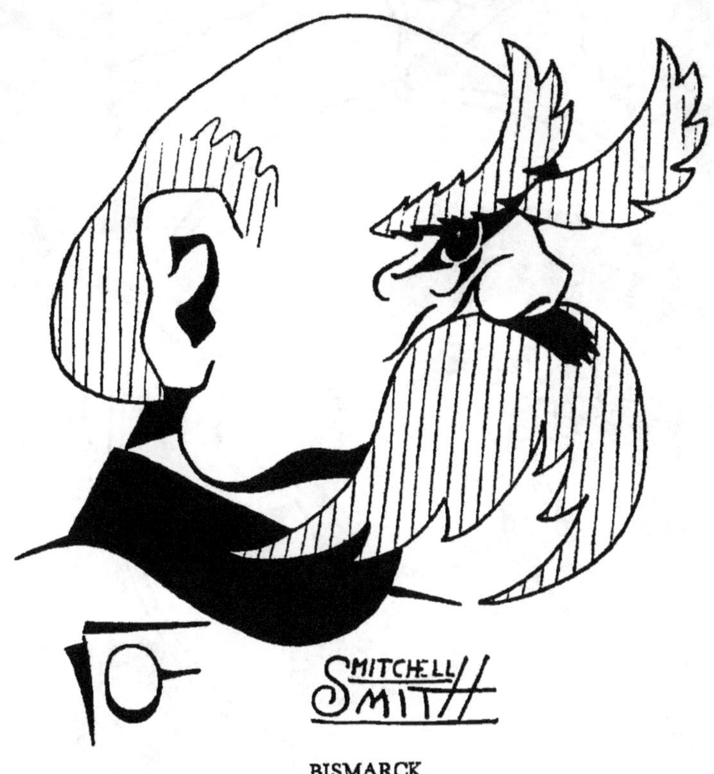

BISMARCK

Poet, John Masefield. Attention is called to the difference in exaggeration of the hair, nose, mustache, and chin. Figure 4 on this plate is a caricature of William Makepeace Thackeray.

In drawing caricatures a good rule to follow is this: first, make a drawing as true to life as possible using little exaggeration; second, study this and make several sketches to determine which features to

COMIC
CARICATURES
"JACK"
MITCHELL SMITH
EXTREME
EXAGGER-
ATION

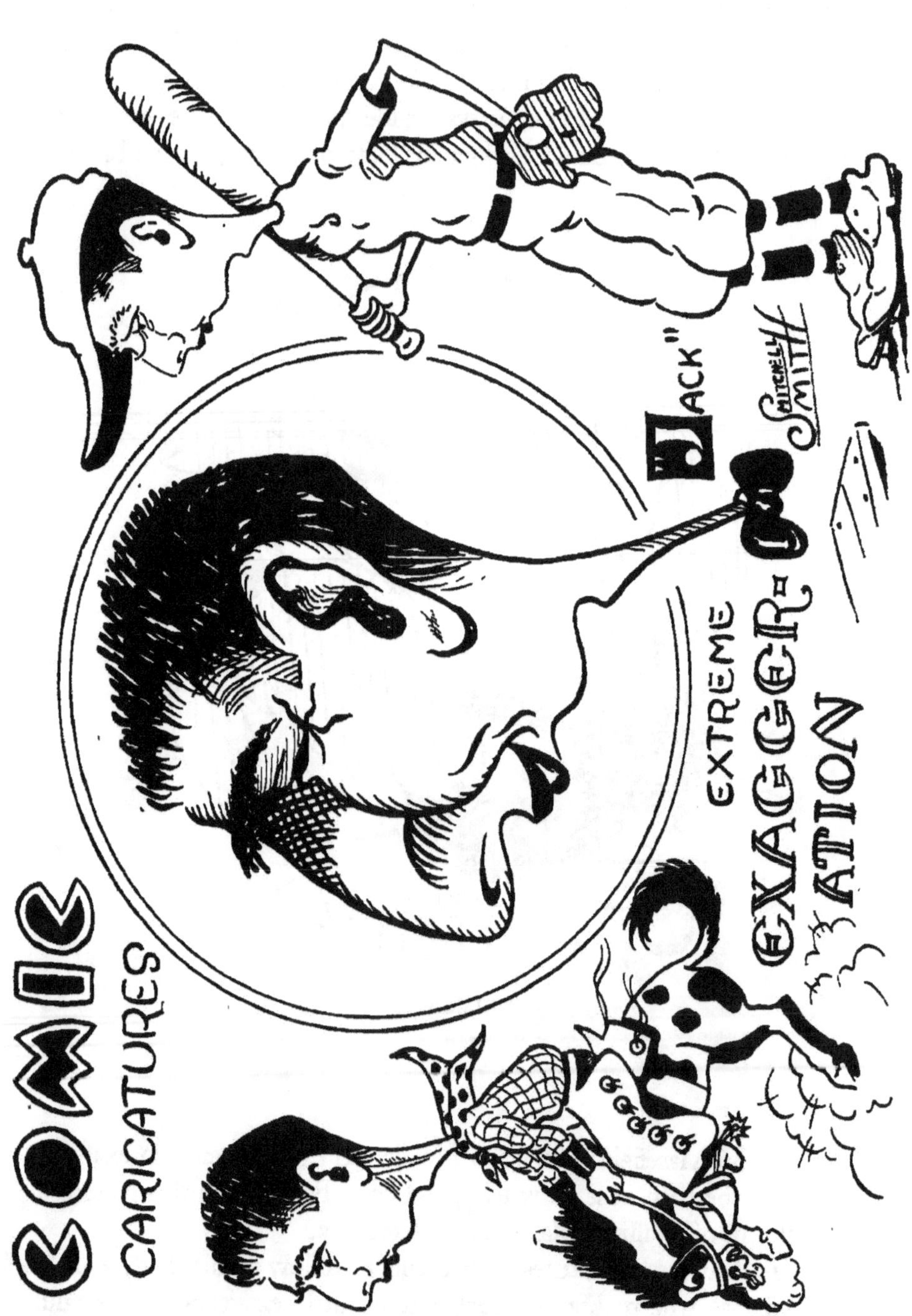

PLATE 8

exaggerate; third, experiment to see which technique is most appropriate for the exaggeration used. If you are drawing from life, make sketches of profile, front, and two-thirds front view. By doing all this sketching and experimenting you can get much better results. Study the caricatures of Howard Thurston on **Plate 15,** for an example of different ways of caricaturing the same person. Also the caricatures on **Plate 8.** Extreme exaggeration was employed in the large head on this plate which gives a humorous effect, and at the same time a fairly good likeness was retained. Also see the two caricatures of General John J. Pershing. **Plate 13.** The chin, jaw, and ear were accentuated most in these drawings.

Expression and exaggeration should also be employed to bring out, or express, the character of the person caricatured. The caricatures of Ex Kaiser William II, Figures 4 and 5, **Plate 3,** are examples of this point. By using a stern expression, and exaggerating the jaw, beard and other features, the artist endeavored to represent a conceited man with a strong will. Likewise, an effort was made to represent the character of Von Hindenburg in the caricatures of him, **Plate 7,** the character of a soldier. There is little exaggeration in Fig. 1. Note how the eyelids droop in this drawing. You will also see that the head is rather square, very strong and fort-like, and naturally suggests squaring up; and certainly the mustache is far too good a chance for exaggeration for the alert and original caricaturist to omit. In Fig. 2, and in the finished drawing you will note that a likeness was retained from Figure 1, while the strong character of the Old Soldier was emphasized, obtaining as a reward for study and sketching a very original caricature of a great German.

There is one **don't**, especially, in exaggeration. Never emphasize deformities, or grave abnormalities. People with deformities are invariably sensitive and no one would want to hurt such an unfortunate person.

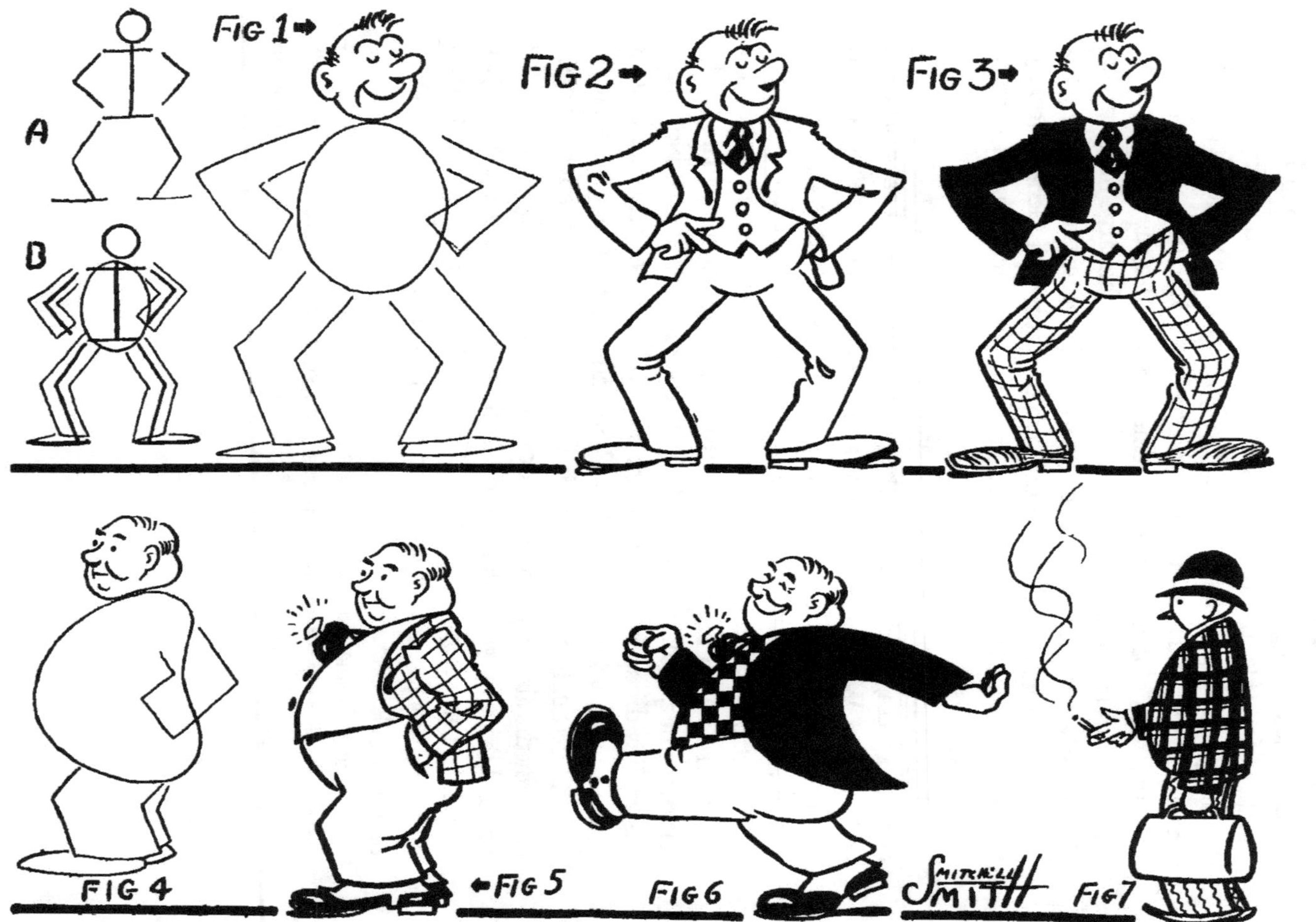

PLATE 9

Chapter V

Comic Figures

Just as a framework is necessary in drawing the head, so is it necessary in drawing a body for the head.

You should know the proportions of a comic figure. Since comic figures may be such gross exaggerations, the proportions of the limbs and torso may vary much in various types, especially between slender and corpulent figures. Note the proportions of Figures 3 and 5 on **Plate 9.** However, in the average figure, the torso and legs are of equal length with the knee midway of the legs, exclusive of the foot. The hands should reach midway of the thigh and the elbow half way of the arm, which makes the elbow near the hip when the arms hang vertically.

For the beginner or amateur, it is better to draw a sort of skeleton for a guide as in Figure A, **Plate 9.** Next block in body, legs and arms. Draw head as in Figure 1. Draw clothing, adding buttons, wrinkles, etc., to give it life, as in Fig. 2, and finish as in Fig. 3. The same procedure is used, in drawing a sideview comic figure. This is illustrated by Figures 4, 5, and 6 on the same plate. Figure 7 shows a different technique.

The most difficult part of the body to draw is the hand. The amateur should give this item a good deal of study and practice, drawing from his own hands as a model, and from other artists' work. It would be wise to clip hands that are good in various positions, from cartoons to keep for reference or models when needed. Quite a lot of humor can be added by well drawn and well placed hands and feet.

Some of the various ways of getting humor in the feet are, by turning the toes out, or in; turning the toes up at the end; exaggerating the foot, and drawing it in other awkward positions. The shoes should be in keeping with the other clothing. That is, a well dressed man has shined shoes, while a hobo has ragged, worn out shoes. The rich man is usually represented with patent leather shoes with white spats as Figure 6, **Plate 9.**

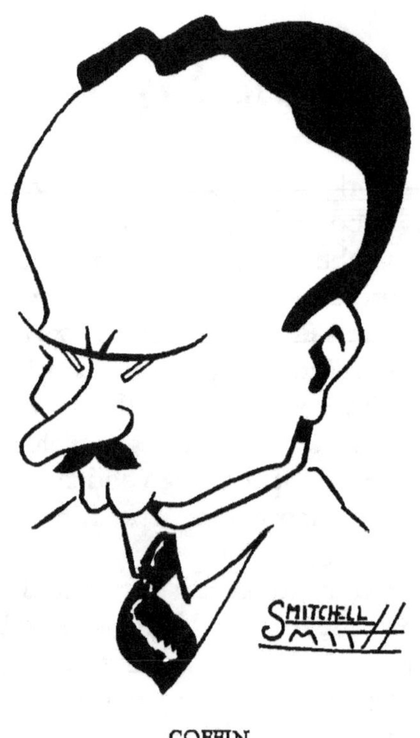

COFFIN

Clothing is really a little difficult, but much diligent study gets fine results here as everywhere else. It should fit the body and should drape naturally to get a good effect. Wrinkles and folds are used for this purpose at the shoulders, elbows, knees, and elsewhere. See examples of this on Plates 9, 10, 11 and 12. Note also how the tie and collar are drawn, the lapels, buttons, button-holes and pockets.

However, a good comic figure must have action and proper shading. These will be treated in the two succeeding chapters.

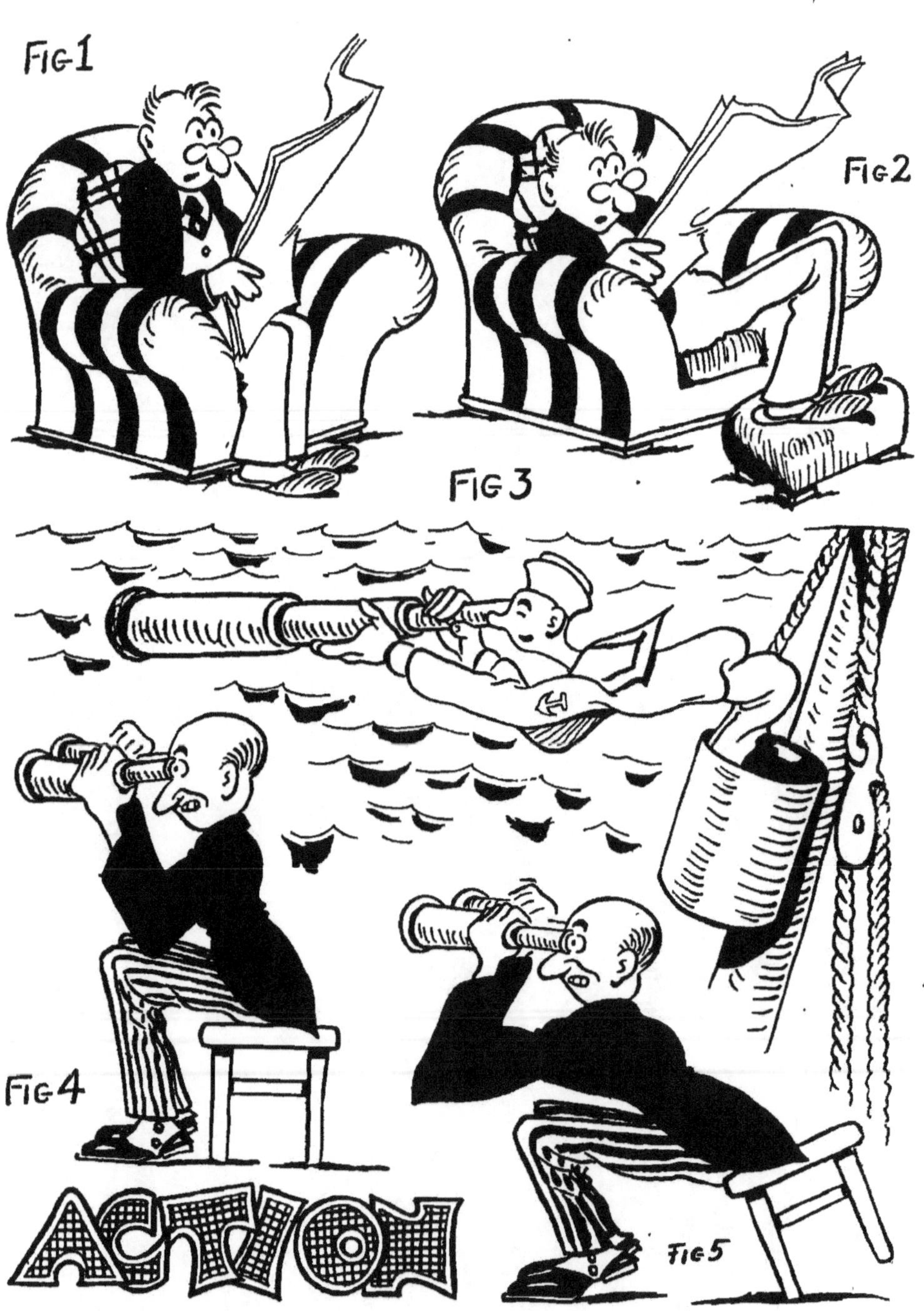

PLATE 10

Chapter VI

Action

Action is all important in cartooning. It is the item that creates greatest interest in a cartoon, or cartoon composition.

Of course action is exaggerated in cartoons just as expressions and forms are exaggerated. In cartoons, even though the figure is not in motion, it is necessary to have what cartoonists term action. On **Plate 10** is illustrated this kind of action. In Figure 1 the man is sitting erect and has little interest about it, except just its comical appearance. In Figure 2 this has been improved by having this man sit more on his spine and moving his knees up by putting his feet on a footstool. Note also the difference in Figures 4 and 5 on **Plate 10**. Figure 3 is another example of action without motion. Do you not think this is a better cartoon than it would be if the sailor was standing erect, and the "crows nest" was larger. However, there is much room for improvement in the drawing of this cartoon.

Action should be suited to expression, and conversely. In anger the hands are tightly closed and shaking, as if threatening to hit something; the feet, or foot stamping the ground, and a general disorder of the hair, hat, cravat, and other clothing. Angles in lines, or between lines help to express disorder. Figure 2, **Plate 12**, might be classed as anger and determination combined.

Appropriate action for **fear** might be as follows: running, or if standing, jumping off the ground; hat flying in air, hair standing on end, and fingers spread wide apart.

The characteristic actions for **stupidity** are, slumped form with hands and feet relaxed, causing them to take awkward positions. Straight and gracefully curved lines express order, or stillness.

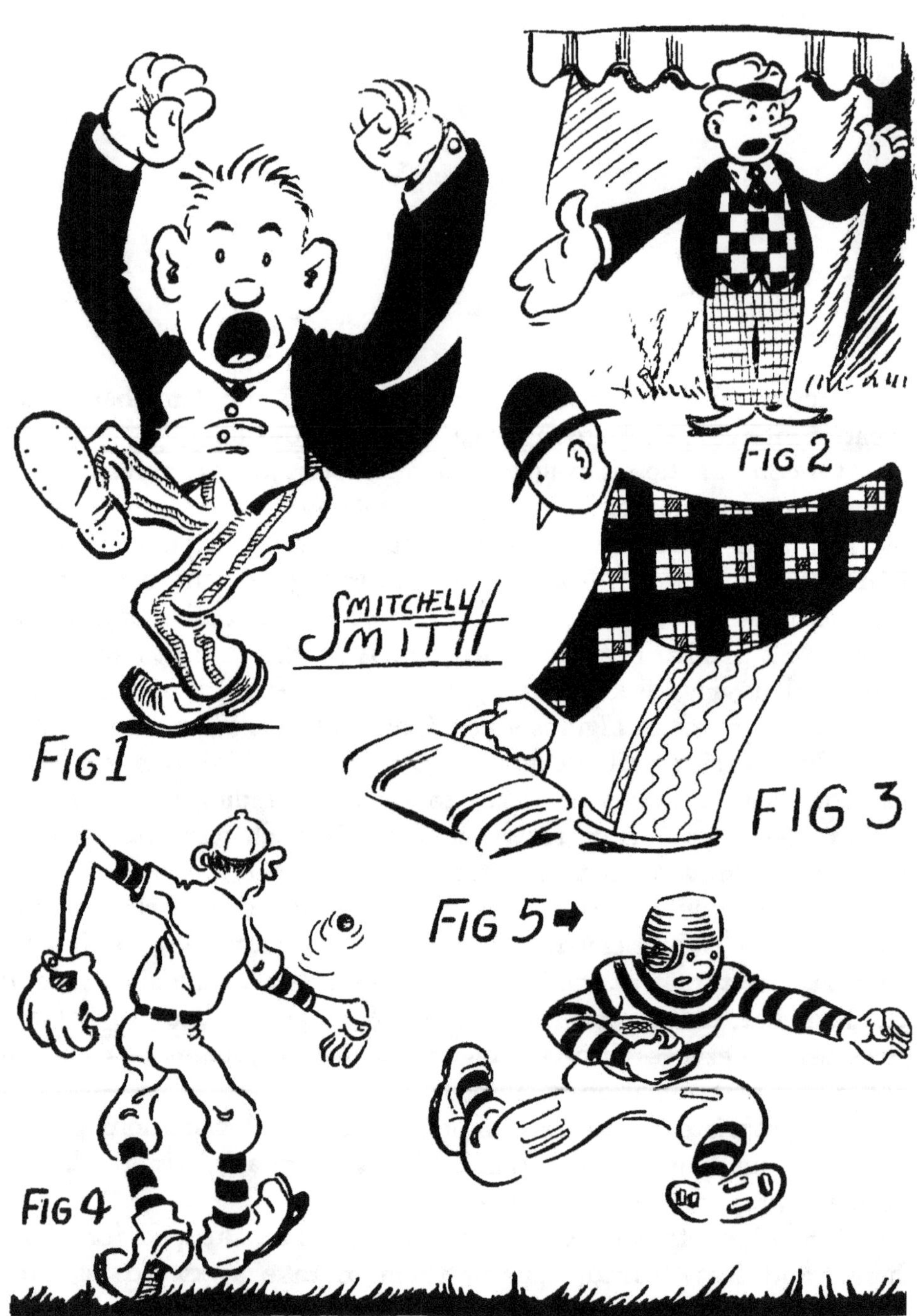

MITCHELL SMITH
FIG 1
FIG 2
FIG 3
FIG 4
FIG 5 ➡

Study the appropriate actions for the various other expressions. You will find some examples in this book. Other good examples of

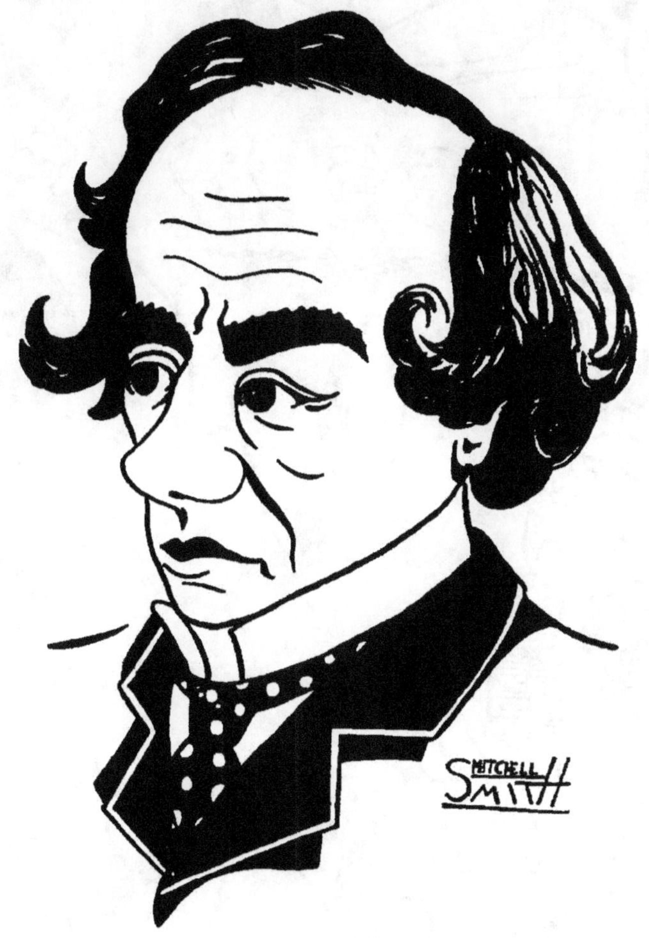

DISRAELI

action you can find in the daily comic strips, especially Popeye and Moon Mullins, and in the cartoons of Herbert Johnson, Tony Sarg, and other top notch cartoonists.

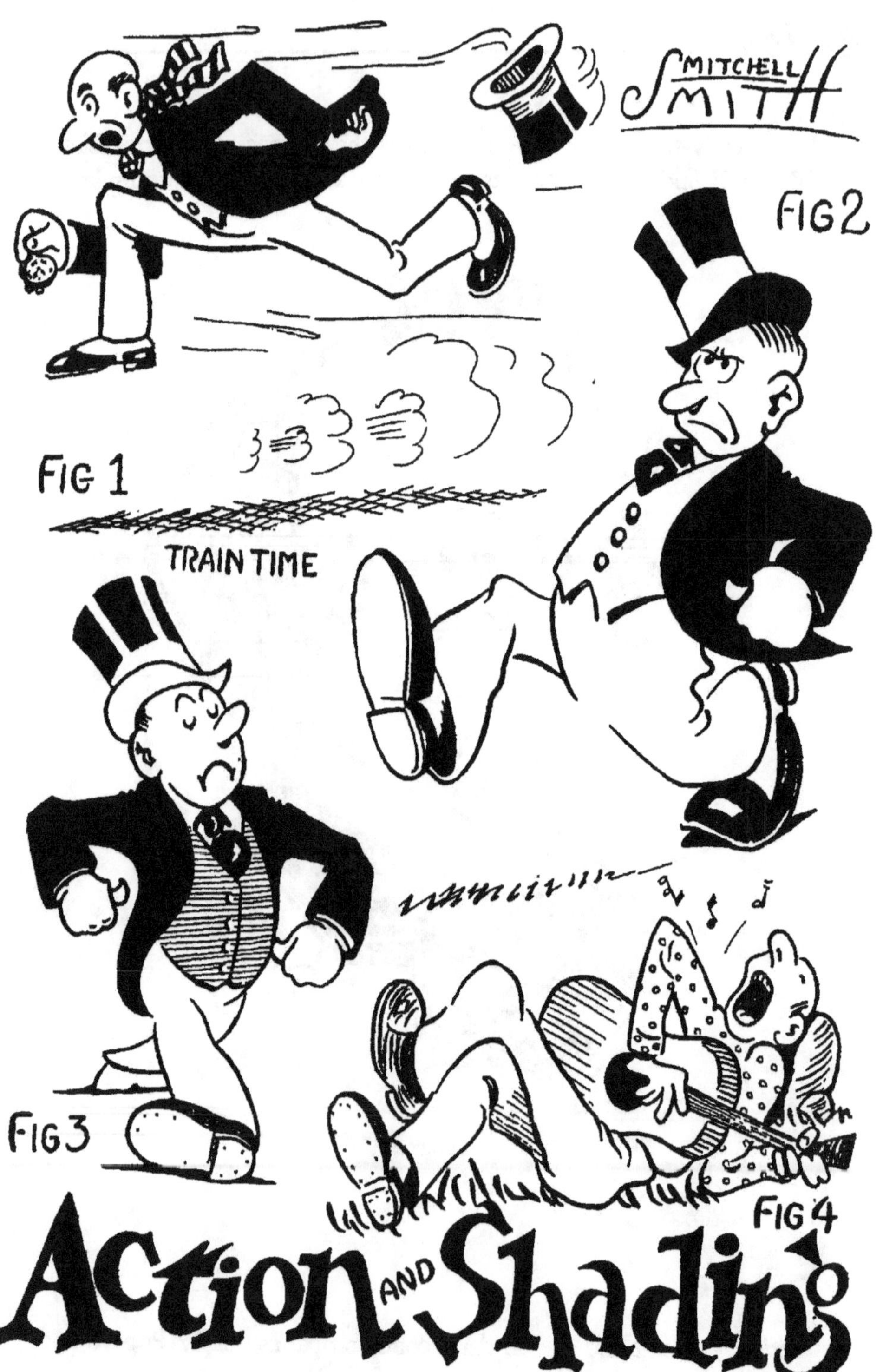

MITCHELL SMITH
FIG 2
FIG 1
TRAIN TIME
FIG 3
FIG 4
Action AND Shading
PLATE 12

In the act of walking, the hands, feet and other parts of the body change position rapidly and this causes a shifting of wrinkles and folds in the clothing. The hands in different positions are necessarily drawn differently, and these details require close study. In walking, the

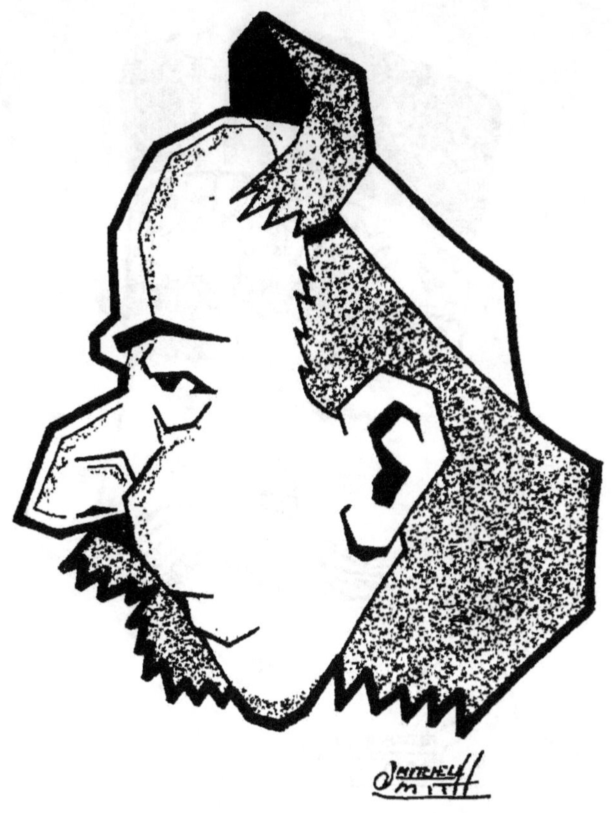

TAFT

forward foot may or may not have the heel resting on the ground, but it is usually drawn straight, while the rear foot is bent at the toes with the heel off the ground. See Figure 2, Action and Shading, **Plate 12.** There are various other details that must be watched closely, such as the weight of clothing, keeping the proper relationship between the arms and legs in action, and others. Note the comical action in the walking figures (2 and 3) on **Plate 12.** Also Figure 6, **Plate 9.**

For running action study Figure 1 on **Plate 12.** Note the action of the arms and legs in running. The elbow is, of course, bent upward

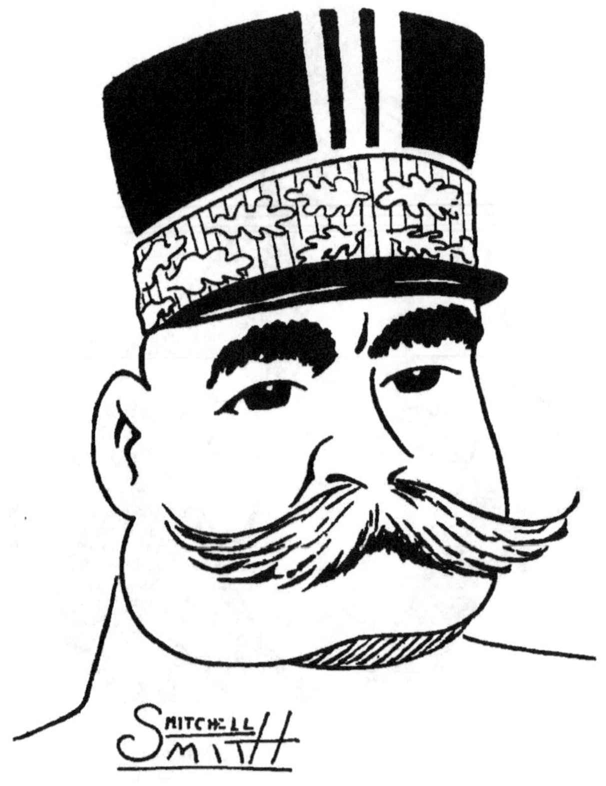

JOFFRE

of the arm in the backward swing, and downward on the forward swing. The knee of the forward leg is bent upward, while that of the other is bent downward. The forward hand is closed, and the other is partly open with the fingers pointing upward. The feet are drawn practically the same as in walking, except that they are off the ground. Drawing them off the ground improves the action a great deal, and is done by simply drawing a shadow underneath, as you may see in the above mentioned drawing. Other details that add to the action are, hat blowing off, tie and coat tails blowing backward, and the dust sucked upward and forward over the shadow, and underneath, and to the rear of the man. Especially note the fine streamlines running back from the feet, and from the head, showing the movement and direction of the hat. The short curved lines to the right of the hat causes an illusion that makes it seem that the hat is also in a twirling motion. In Fig. 4 on this same plate see the notes flying from the singing man's mouth.

The front and two-thirds front view figures in motion are drawn somewhat in perspective. For this foreshortening is employed. If one stands in front of you and points his hand and arm at you, you can not see the length of the arm, but you will see the arm in foreshortened position. The hand will also appear larger in comparison to the arm because it is nearer the eye of the observer. So in the above mentioned positions—motion of the front and two-thirds front figures—the hand and foot in front appear larger. An example of this is the feet of Figure 3 on **Plate 12.** For an example of hands in perspective you are referred to Figure 2 on **Plate 11.** Also use heavy lines for the nearer objects and conversely for the more distant objects.

Analyze the action of Figures 1, 3, 4, and 5 on **Plate 11.** Figure 1 was meant to represent the excitable, shouting type of baseball fan instructing the player in what to do next. The use of skeletons in draw-ing comic figures as explained in the preceding chapter, is doubly useful in acquiring good action.

Keep the weight of the body balanced properly on the feet. In Figure 3 mentioned immediately above, note how the body is balanced on the feet. If the legs were in a vertical position here, then the hand would have to support part of the weight of the body, which it is not doing here, but is only picking up the brief case.

MODERNISTIC
HEADS FROM RECENT PHOTOS
GEN. JOHN. J. PERSHING
MITCHELL SMITH
$AM IN$ULL

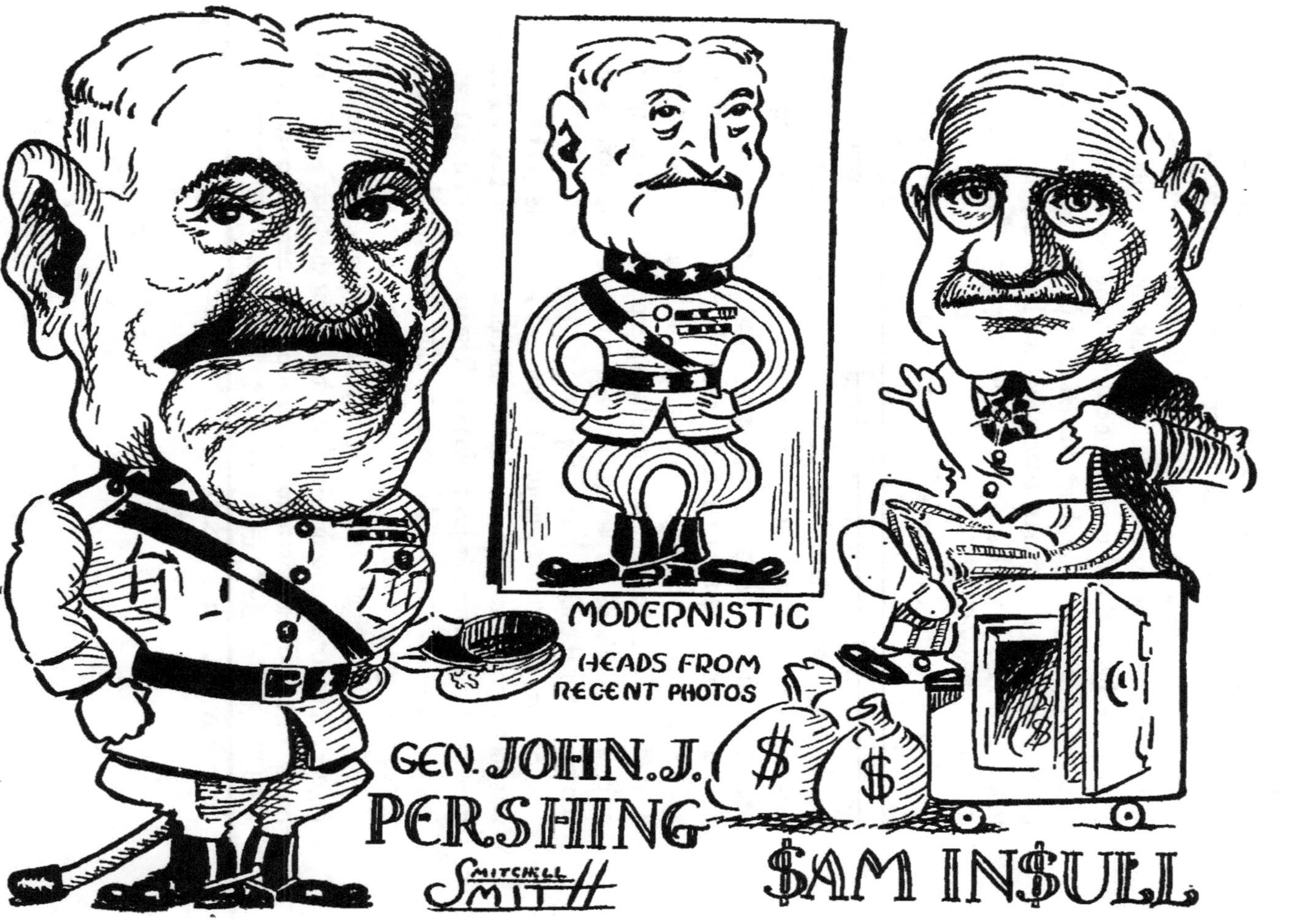

PLATE 13

Chapter VII

Shading and Shadows

Shading is employed to put tone and life into cartoons. In shading the artist must take into consideration the purpose of the cartoon, and the proper technique to be used in the cartoon. When it is consistent with the technique and purpose of the cartoon, it is advisable to employ a variety of shading. For example, say the coat should be solid black, the trousers striped, and the vest shaded with parallel lines.

The different methods of shading are, solid black, stripes, cross hatch, plaids, dots, checks, and stipple or spatter. **Plates 9, 11 and 12** illustrate these various styles of shading. Suitable shading gives a cartoon a professional appearance. Lettering pens or a small brush are used for making large stripes or for solid black areas. Sometimes stripes are not drawn solid black, but are only shaded with a fine pen. Figure 1, **Plate 11** is an example. Figure 2 illustrates checks and Fig. 3, plaid and wriggly stripes. In Figure 4 note how the socks are drawn. There is no outline of the white parts. Note also how the white spats are drawn on **Plate 12.** Also how the shoes and hats are drawn, shaded, and highlighted.

Shading helps to express character. A cartoon of a tramp would naturally be shaded quite differently from one of a rich man; and a cartoon of a cowboy would be shaded differently from either the rich man or the tramp; due to the different type, style, color, weave, and material of the clothing.

Shadows are also very important in drawing cartoons and caricatures. On the various plates in this book note how the cartoonist has handled the shadows. The caricatures on **Plate 7** are good examples of shadows on the head. Your attention is called to the shadows under eyebrows, under upper eyelids, at wrinkles, under nose, mustache and

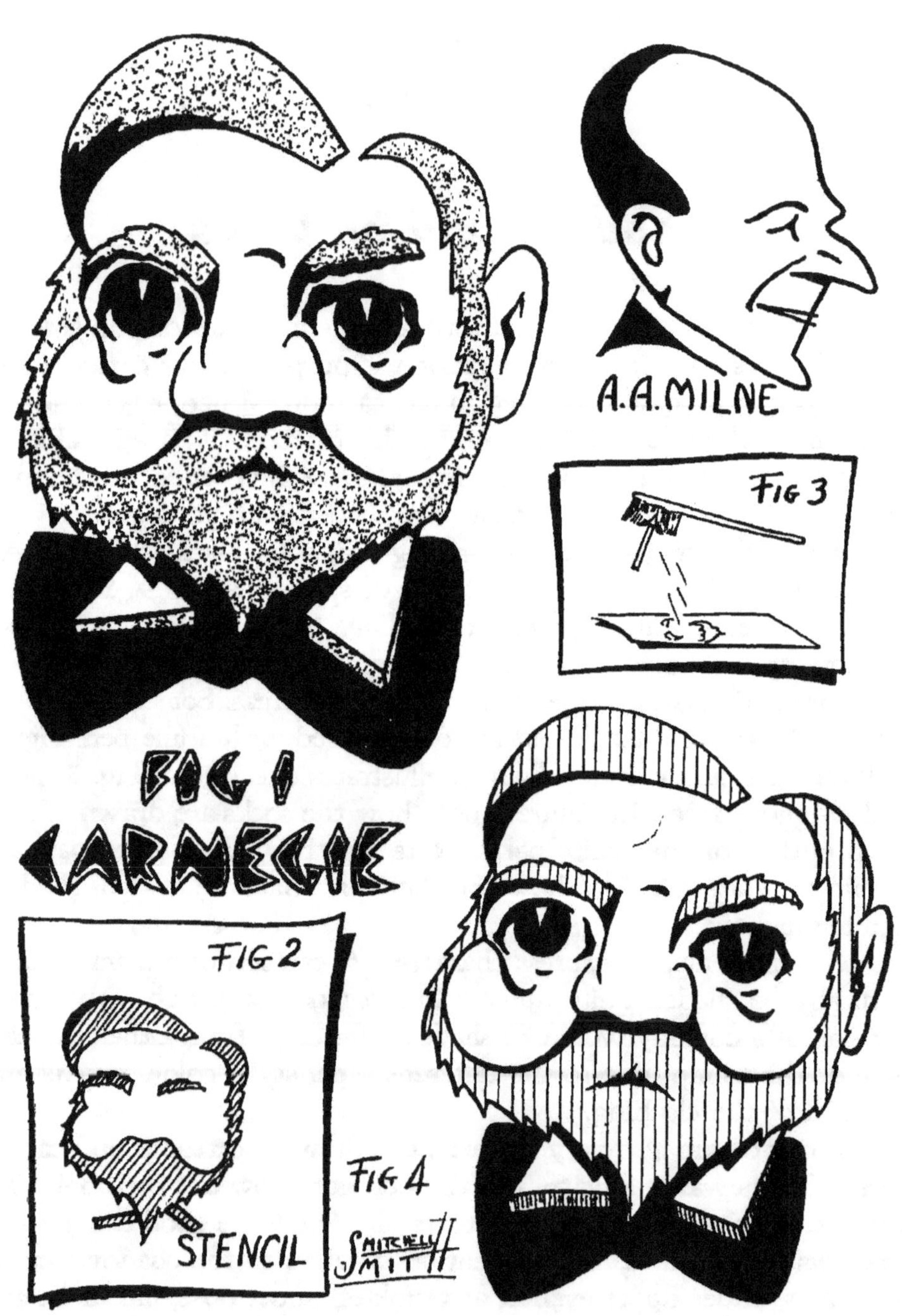
A.A.MILNE
FIG 3
FIG 1
CARNEGIE
FIG 2
FIG 4
STENCIL
MITCHELL SMITH

chin; and in the completed full figure caricature at the right, the shadow under the coat on the trousers. These shadows aid in giving the drawings depth or perspective, by causing the features to stand out more prominently.

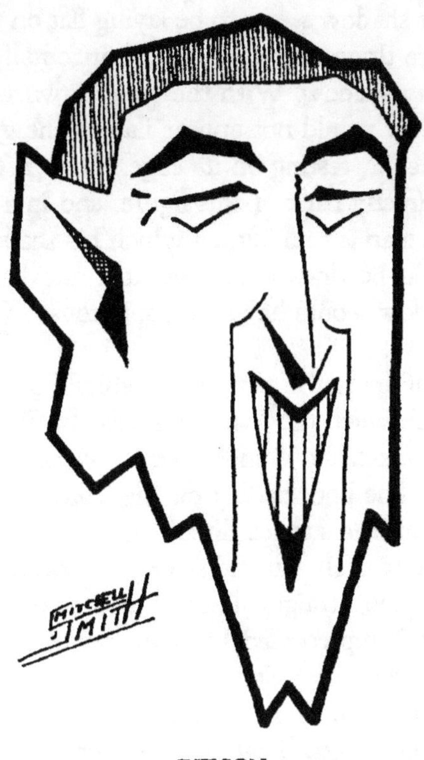

WILSON

In the drawings on **Plates 11** and **12** are other applications of shadows. They appear under the collar, lapels, buttons, pocket flaps, vest, coat tails, belts, trouser bottoms, and under the spats on the shoes, and under the shoes. Shadows under the shoes aid in making the feet appear in contact with the ground. The right foot of the football player, Figure 5, **Plate 11**, would appear on the ground if an appropriately drawn shadow was drawn just back of the toe. As it is, both feet are off the ground.

Just as shadows are used to make the feet contact the ground, so are they used to show that they are off the ground. Figure 1 on **Plate 12** illustrates this point. Notice that these cross hatch lines are drawn so that the shadow seems to be laying flat on the ground. If the shading lines were drawn vertically and horizontally they would not make a satisfactory shadow. With the lines drawn vertically and horizontally the shadow would not appear flat on the ground, but would appear as if in the air, resting on its edge. Now if there was a house or board fence directly back of this figure, and in a line parallel with the direction this man is running, on which his shadow was cast, then the shadow would be drawn with vertical and horizontal lines. In that case the shadow would have the approximate shape of this figure in silhouette.

Shadows that are not in perspective should conform to the shape of the object from which the shadow is cast. In Figure 3 on **Plate 10**, notice that the black shadow under the crows nest follows the curvature of the mast. The line shading on the mast, crows nest, and telescope also bring out the surface direction, or curvature of the surface on which the shadows fall. Curved strokes are essential in representing rounded objects, and straight lines in representing plane surfaces. Surface direction is represented by lines drawn in the same general direction as the surface direction.

The same direction of light and shadow should be maintained throughout a composition. That is, if one object in the composition is lighted from the East with the shadow cast Westward, all other objects in the same composition should be lighted and shaded accordingly from the same direction. This is an error often made by beginners. Although absolute accuracy is not necessary in cartoons as it is in the more serious arts, gross incongruities will ruin an otherwise good cartoon. Therefore, the beginner should watch carefully for such errors and correct them.

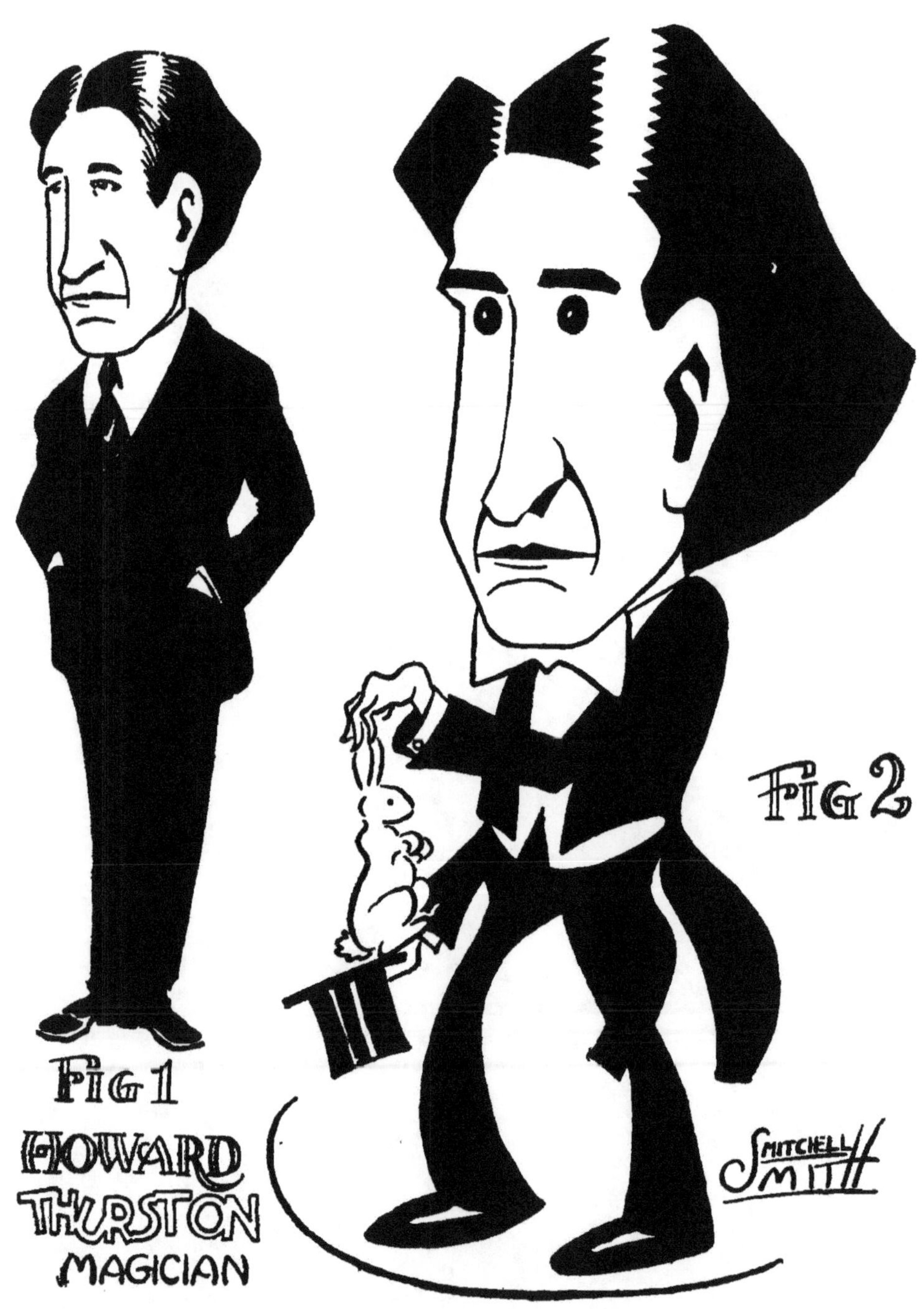

PLATE 15

Chapter VIII

Technique

Technique is the method of performance in art; in other words, the style or method used in producing a work of art.

In caricaturing the purpose of the drawing may influence the technique of the artist, or rather may influence the artist in choosing the technique. For example, a caricature drawn for newspaper reproduction is usually drawn with pen and ink lines similar to the drawings on **Plates 8, 13,** and **16.** Some artists use Lithographic Pencils on a specially prepared, pebbled surfaced board. Ripley of "Believe It Or Not" fame produces his drawings by this method. Wash is seldom used in this country for newspaper drawings.

A large number of caricatures are used in sports cartoons for newspapers. Sports cartoons may of course illustrate various sports, such as: boxing, baseball, basketball, football, golf, hunting, fishing, horseback riding, and others. Often in these humorous drawings the central figure is drawn with a small body and a large caricatured head, somewhat as the caricatures on **Plates 8, 13,** and **16.** Around this central figure are drawn smaller action figures illustrating one or more sports. Names, dates, comments and other lettering and details are placed so as to make a good composition.

Somewhat the same technique is employed in political cartoons, in which Presidents, Vice-Presidents, Senators, Congressmen, Cabinet Members, Governors, and other statesmen and prominent men may be caricatured. Here again the purpose of the drawing may determine the way it should be drawn. By "purpose of the cartoon" is meant whether it is intended to aid or injure the one caricatured. If it is to harm the caricatured, naturally he will be represented differently from what he would otherwise. Figures 1, 4, and 5 on **Plate 3** represents the Ex-Kaiser as a rather stern, ruthless, and strong willed monarch. There is no doubt that he is stern and strong willed, but not so terrible as these caricatures represent him. Figures 2 and 3 on the same

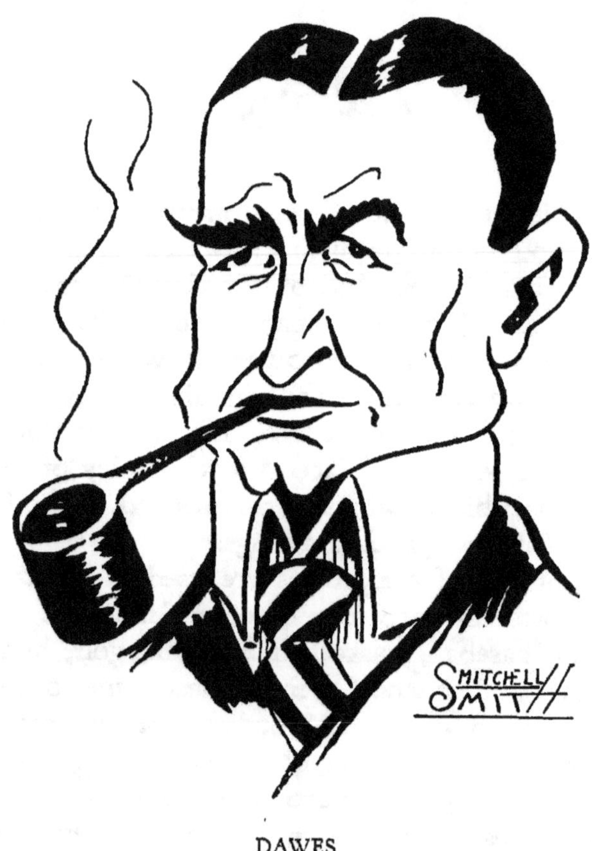

DAWES

plate represent more of a kindly old gentleman, but even in them one can discern that he is no weak person by his stern features and prominent jaw. It should be interesting for the student to study some of the caricatures of Thomas Nast, if he can acquire reproductions of same, even though cartoonists of today do not go as far as Nast did.

Humor is very important in newspaper cartoons. There are three ways of putting this quality in them, and these are, action, expression, and exaggeration. A cartoon is rather flat and uninteresting if it lacks these qualities.

Some of the caricatures in this book might be termed modernistic.

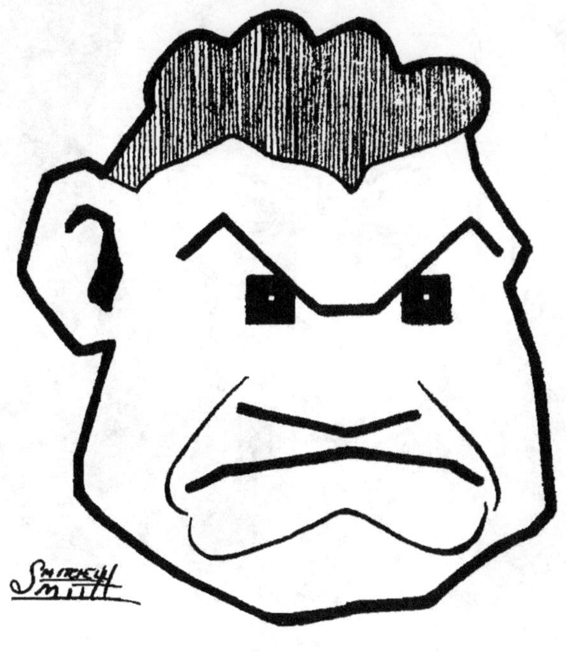

DEMPSEY

Especially the caricatures of Hindenburg, Carnegie, R. T. Coffin, Marshal Foch, Lorado Taft, Charles Darwin, and Jack Dempsey. There are also others of this type. Some of these are spattered; some are drawn with straight lines; some with curved lines; and some with light and very heavy lines which were made with a lettering pen. The character of the person and the shape of the features has determined the technique used, for which they were most adapted. It is assumed that the above named caricatures are best as they are, although caricatures of the same men might be drawn differently. The caricatures

SMITCHELL SMITH
GREATEST
PIANIST
FAMOUS
POLISH
STATESMAN,
COMPOSER
AND
PIANIST
BORN 1860
IGNACE PADEREWSKI

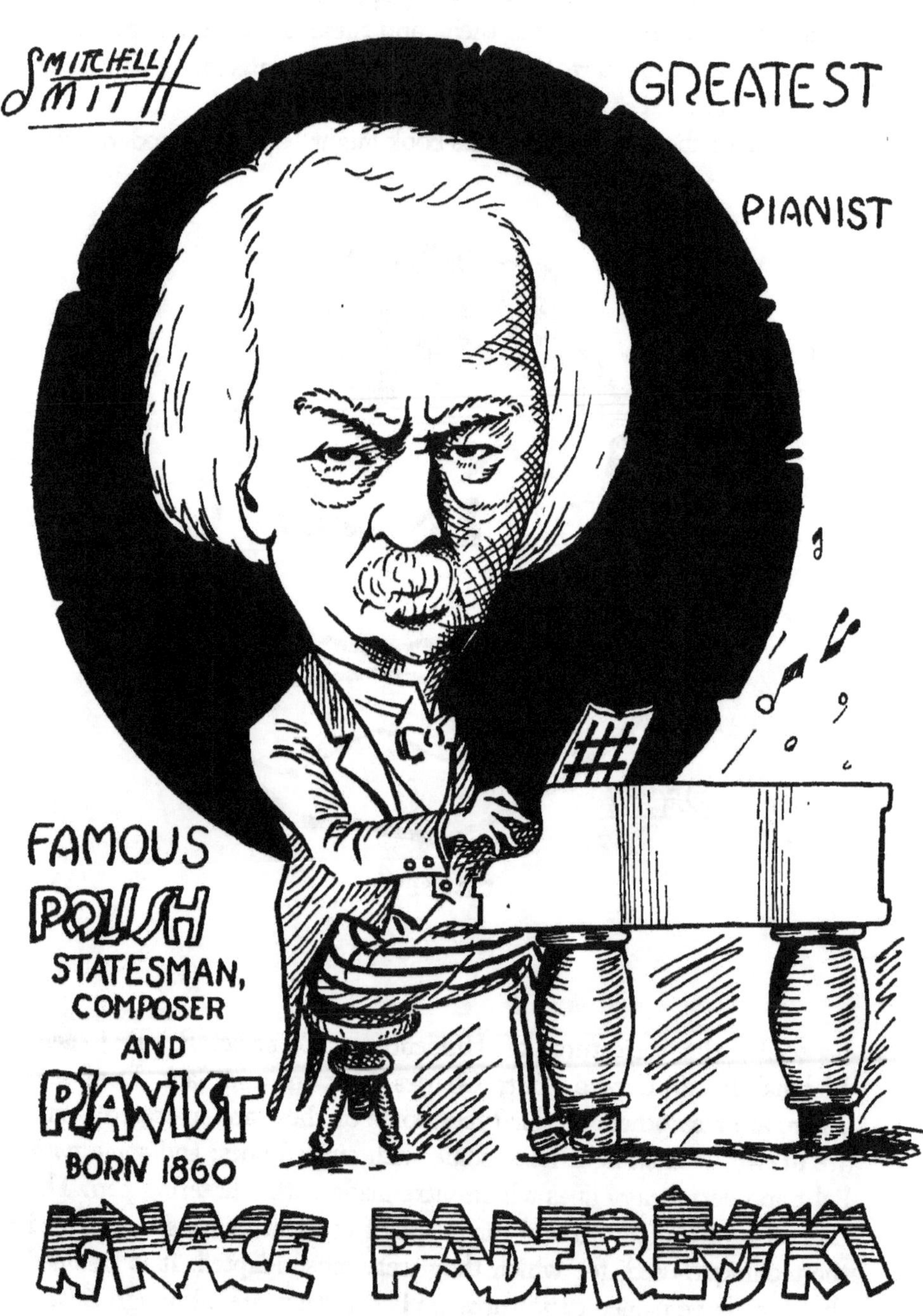

PLATE 16

of Woodrow Wilson might be drawn with curved lines, but it would perhaps not be as good as this drawing and would lack its originality. However, the drawing of R. T. Coffin could hardly be drawn well with straight lines due to the round face. Neither could that of Carnegie, for the same reason. They are simply not adapted to the techniques employed in some of the other drawings.

If the head is drawn in a modernistic technique, the body, if a body is used, should be in the same style. This was done in the caricatures of Hindenburg and Howard Thurston.

Since stipple, or rather spatter has been employed in a number of drawings in this book, it seems appropriate to explain here the procedure for this method of drawing.

The large caricature of Carnegie on **Plate 14** is spattered on the hair, eyebrows, and beard. As one can readily see, first an outline drawing is made. If it is suitable to be spattered, a stencil is cut for this purpose. To make this stencil, place a sheet of transparent paper, sufficiently large, over the drawing and trace the outlines of the areas to be stippled (spattered). If transparent paper is unavailable, the drawing may be traced with carbon or graphite paper. In this way the drawing to be traced would be placed on top. The next step is to cut out the portions to be spattered from the stencil, as the shaded area in Figure 2, **Plate 14**. A single edge razor blade, or a pocket knife is very useful to cut the stencil where it is inconvenient to cut with shears.

Place the stencil over the outline drawing so that the cut out portions register perfectly with the outlines of the drawing to be stippled. Thumb tack the two together, or place weights on them to hold them in the desired position. Pour a small quantity of drawing ink in a saucer or similar receptacle. An old tooth brush is used for spattering. Dip the brush lightly in the ink and draw the bristles across a coin or other suitable object as illustrated in Figure 3, **Plate 14**. A little practice will teach you to do this properly.

Some solid black should also be used with this spattered shading to give contrast and thereby improve the drawing as a whole. In the Hindenburg Caricature, **Plate 7**, spatter shading has been used on the body and in the lettering underneath, as the same technique should be employed consistently throughout an entire drawing or composition, as stated previously in this chapter.

Quite often wash is used in caricaturing. For this technique, Lamp Black water color is used with a water color brush. First an outline drawing is made with a pen and black waterproof drawing ink on water color paper. Then the wash is applied with a camels hair brush. Additional washes are used for the darker parts, and an effort is made to blend the two values.

The frontispiece is a reproduction of an air-brushed caricature study of George Arliss by Eddie Burgess. This drawing was made for a theatrical display, and the artist has produced something original and very good. This caricature has originality, humor, and most important of all, it has a fair likeness of the subject caricatured.

Caricatures of some subjects are better drawn in one technique, while others are best caricatured in another technique. The only way to determine the best technique for any particular subject is by good judgment, and experiment.

 Caricaturing

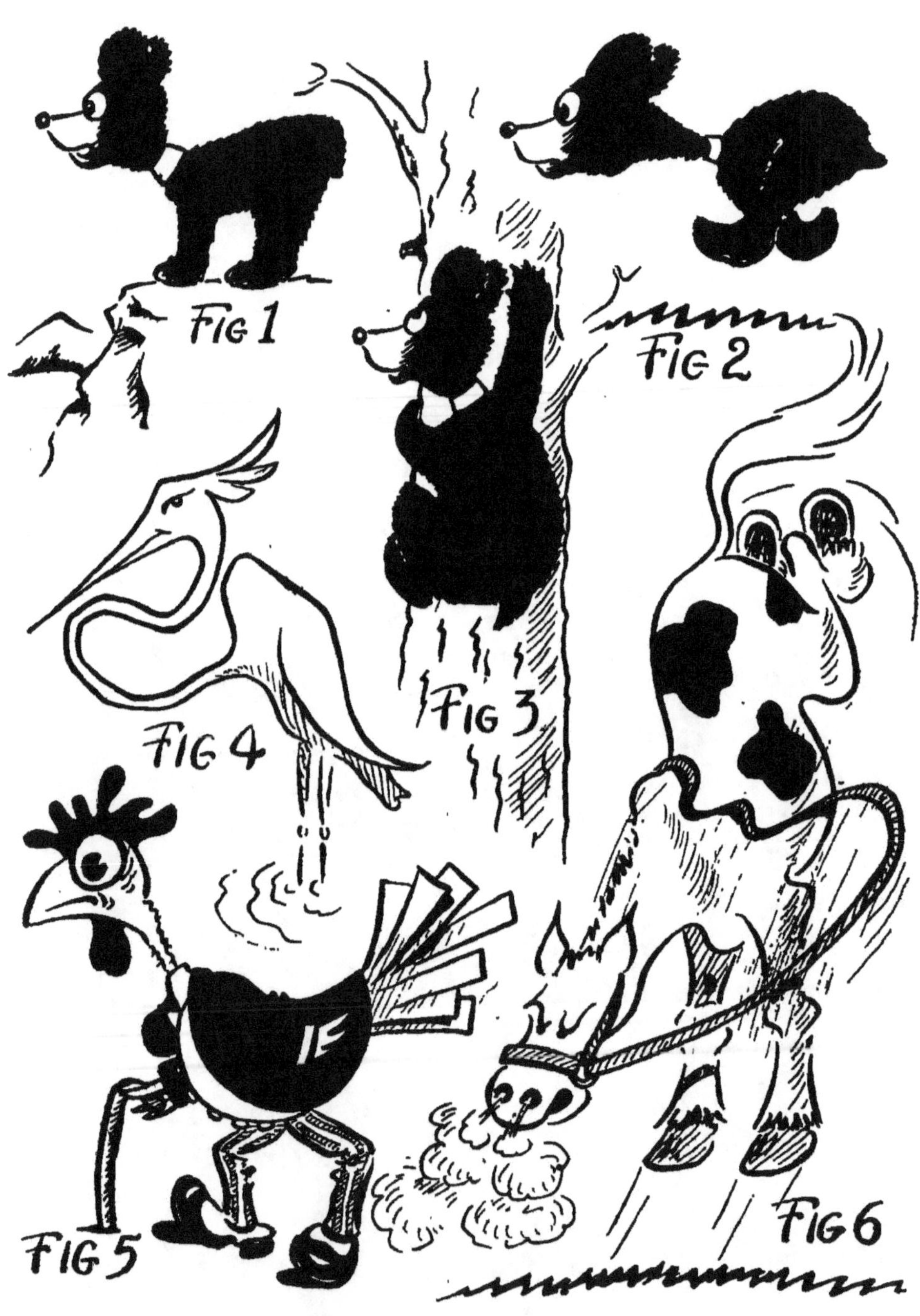

PLATE 17

Chapter IX

Animals

The caricaturing of animals should be learned along with the caricaturing of the human form. Cartoons of animals are frequently used in newspaper drawings; especially political cartoons, in which they are employed as symbols of political parties, or of the various nations of the World.

These symbolic animals and the things they represent are listed immediately below. The donkey is the symbol of the Democratic Party. The elephant represents the Republican Party; G. O. P. (Grand Old Party). Other symbolic animals are, the Tammany Tiger, the British Lion, the Chinese Dragon, the American Eagle, and the Russian Bear. Animals are sometimes used as symbols for ball teams. Wildcats, Panthers, Tigers, Bulldogs, and others are employed for this purpose.

Practically the same rules used in caricaturing the human body are used in caricaturing animals. The greatest difference is that of form. As in the case of the human form, the forms of animals are exaggerated; the most prominent features being accentuated most. Action and expression are also exaggerated. The expressions of animals are practically the same as that of humans and the same rules apply, although it is sometimes more difficult because of the difference in the form of the head, from the form of the human head and face.

The action in the movements of animals is necessarily different from human action; especially in the quadrupeds. The actions of walking, running and galloping are essentially the same in all animals, except apes and other bipeds. These actions are rather difficult to describe, and should be studied from life, and from the work of artists who are especially good in the draftsmanship of animals.

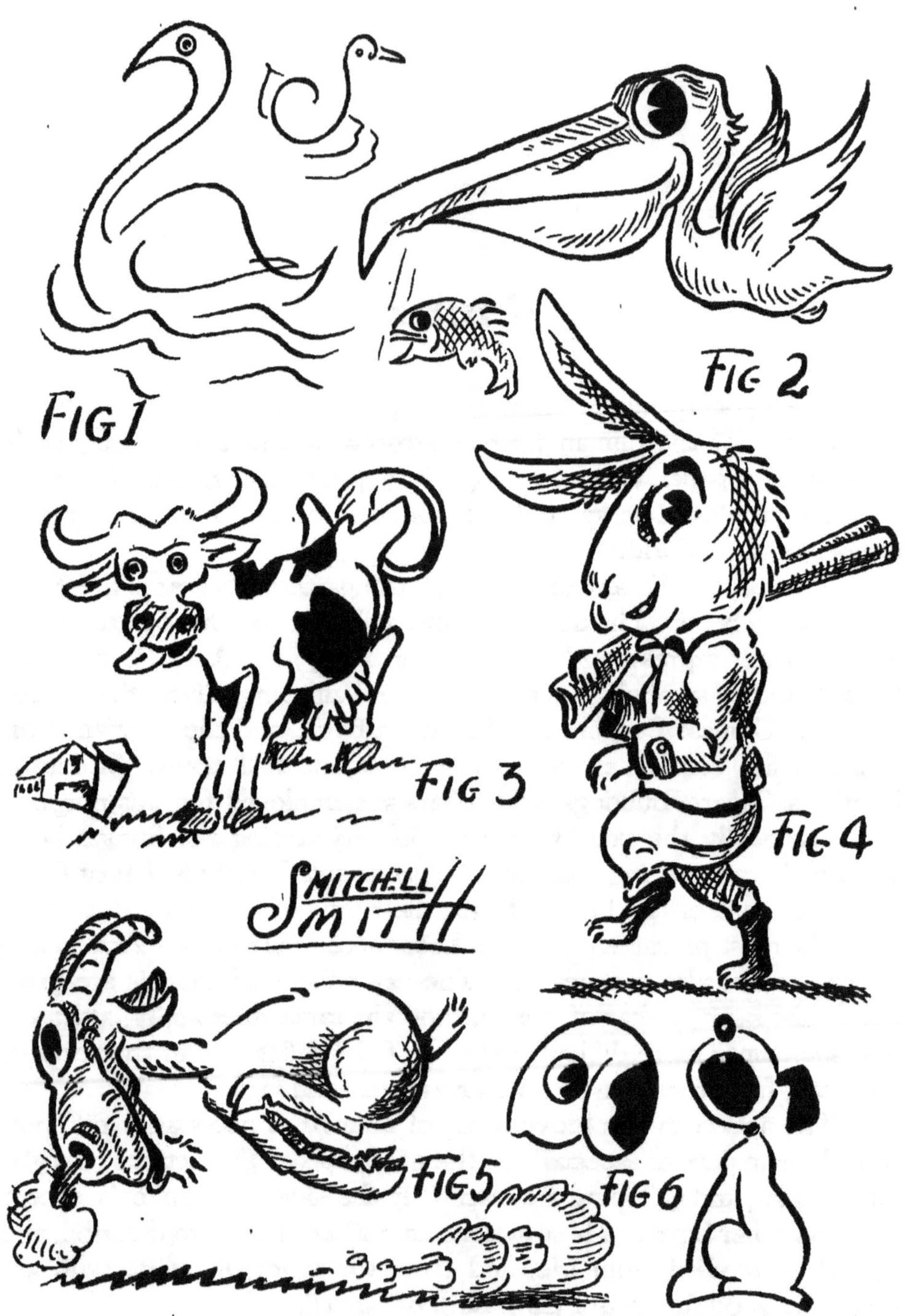

PLATE 18

In walking, quadrupeds only have two feet on the ground at one time. Take the horse for an example. If the right rear foot is forward and on the ground, then the right front foot is slightly off the ground just in front of the rear foot. At the same time the left rear foot is

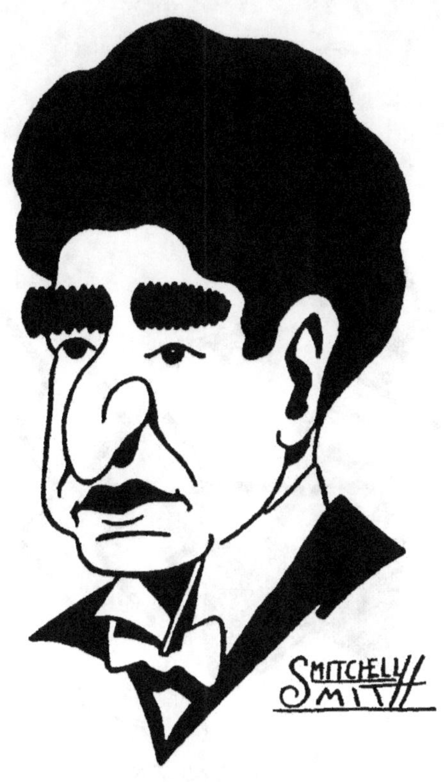

LHEVINNE

lifted to be brought forward, and the left front foot is also lifted and moving forward. The head is moved alternately up and down with each step, and the tail also varies in action. These descriptions can only impart to one a general idea, and the principles of the various actions, for as stated previously, to get the actions correctly drawn one must use a good drawing for a model, or else draw from life.

Running action is similar to walking except movements are faster. The running or trotting action is little used in cartoons because galloping gives a better effect.

In galloping the feet are moved in pairs. Both pairs are either under the body, or the front pair are more forward, although they may

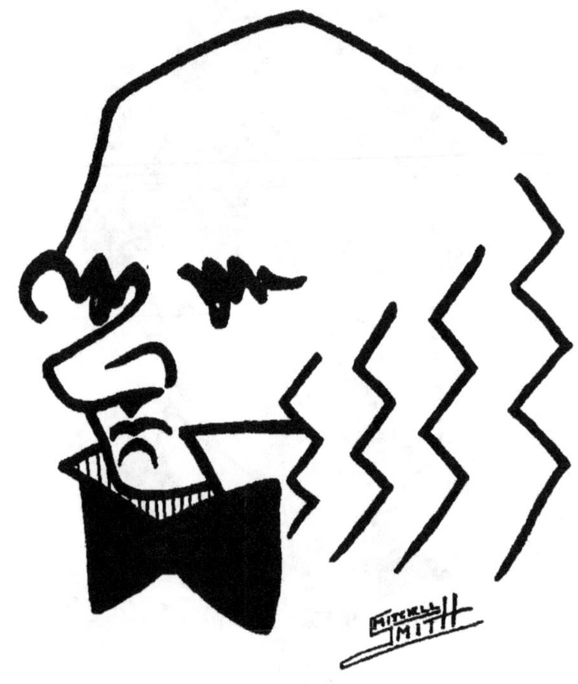

DARWIN

still be under the body, and the rear feet are extended to the rear. All feet are off the ground with shadow underneath to improve the action. The head is thrust forward with the nose held higher, considering the height of the head. The mane and tail are blown to rearward. Galloping action is illustrated by Figure 5, **Plate 18**, and Figure 2, **Plate 17**.

There is also the action of standing, Fig. 1, **Plate 17**; climbing, Fig. 3; bucking, Fig. 6, and the bronco on **Plate 8**. Swimming and flying are illustrated by Figures 1 and 2 on **Plate 18.** The pelican in Figure 2 is also an example of accentuating the most noticeable features. The fish which has just escaped from the pelican's beak adds interest to the drawing.

Quite often comic animals are represented wearing human apparel; such as hats, spectacles, suits and shoes; and quadrupeds are given the same action as bipeds. Examples of this are Figure 4, **Plate 18,** and Figure 5, **Plate 17.** Other examples are Mickey Mouse and Felix the Cat.

In caricaturing animals the style of drawing is influenced by the purpose for which it is drawn. For example, a donkey drawn in a political cartoon intended to aid the Democratic Party should be sleek and fat with a merry expression; on the other hand, the donkey in a cartoon for the aid of the Republican Party, or to criticize the Democrats should be drawn with a starved, moth-eaten, down-and-out appearance. The expression should be consistent with the style; such as, stupidity: ears drooping and eyelids heavy and partly closed. A donkey drawn to illustrate a book for children might be represented quite differently from either of the two above. You should always consider the purpose of a cartoon and choose the style accordingly.

However, you must also consider the idea to be expressed. A donkey drawn to criticize the Democratic Party might be drawn sleek and fat if it was intended to criticize the party for reckless spending. You need only to use good judgment in determining what to do and must have a basic knowledge of a thing to be capable of using the best judgment. Of course there are exceptions to this rule, but as a general rule it is quite true.

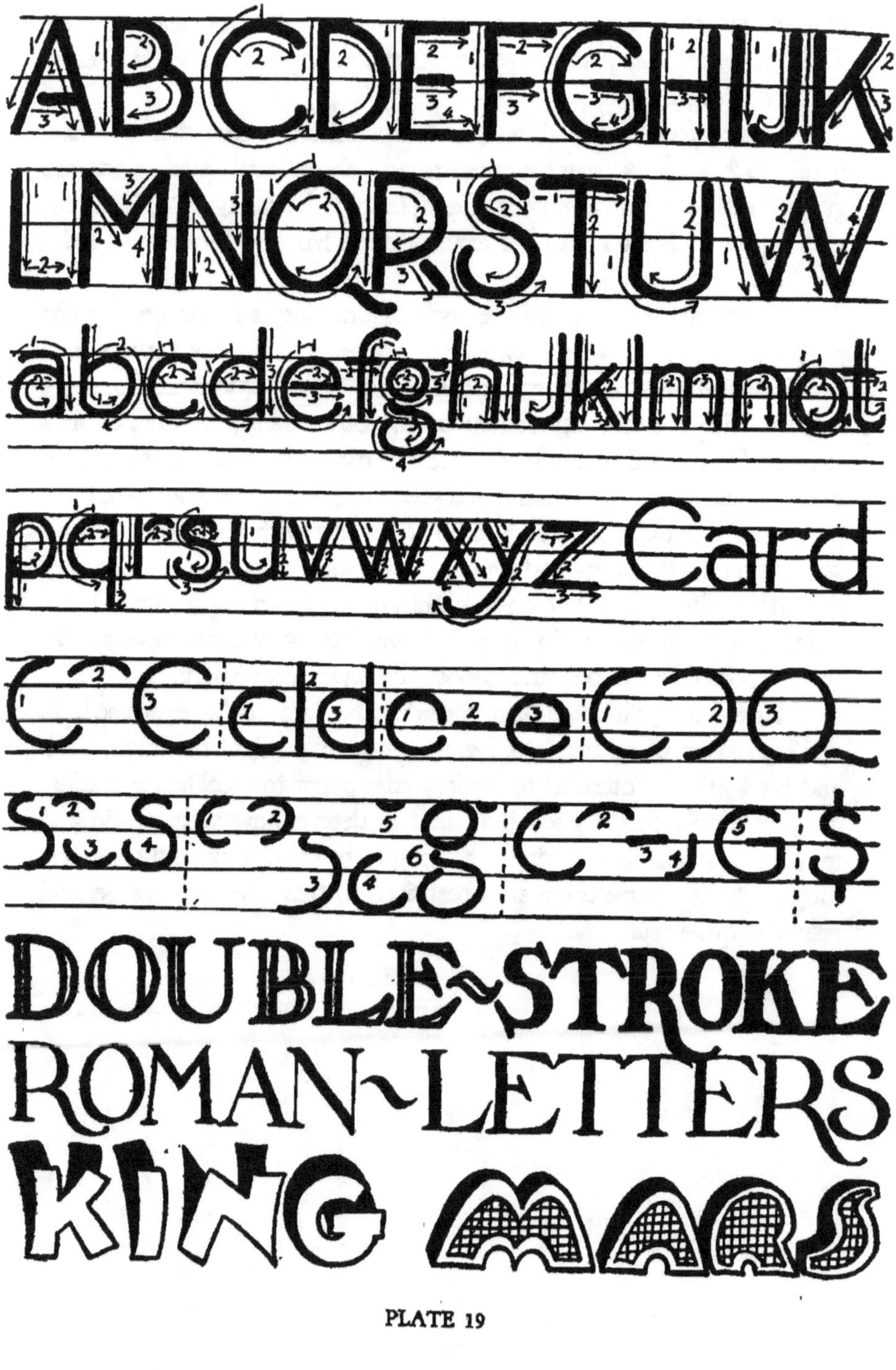

ABCDEFGHIJK
LMNOPQRSTUVW
abcdefghijklmnot
pqrsuvwxyz Card

C C Cclde—e CDQ

S Sc S g C—G$

DOUBLE~STROKE
ROMAN~LETTERS
KING MARS

Chapter X

Lettering

Lettering is necessary in most forms of commercial art. The student of Commercial Art, Cartooning, or Caricaturing should acquire some knowledge of this subject. Therefore, this short chapter is included so that the student may know the first steps in lettering. Only the most important points in lettering can be treated here, for lettering is a long subject, enough for a book in itself. In fact there are many books published on lettering and the student is advised to obtain a good one on this subject and learn to do good lettering.

Lettering is really not very difficult, but it requires a knowledge of the various strokes, guide lines, forms of letters, and the materials for same. However, practice is necessary to acquire the dexterity required to do good lettering.

In pen and ink cartoons and caricatures, lettering is often exaggerated, just as the drawings are exaggerated. It should also be of an appropriate style to harmonize with the technique of the drawings. Note how this was done on the plates of this book; especially, the word "Carnegie" on **Plate 14**. Note the word "Hindenburg" on **Plate 7**. Block letters were used to harmonize with the caricature, which is also somewhat of a block form. This caricature shows strength of character, and block letters suggest strength and power, so it is apparent that this style of lettering was the most appropriate for this drawing. The shading on the letters is also made to match the drawing.

For lettering you should have lettering pens in various sizes and styles, black lettering ink, a T square for making vertical and horizontal guide lines, and pencils, paper, and other materials used for caricaturing.

75

There are three classes of letters used by letter craftsmen. They are, Gothic, Roman, and Text. Gothic letters are those having the elementary strokes of even width. The four top lines on **Plate 19** are

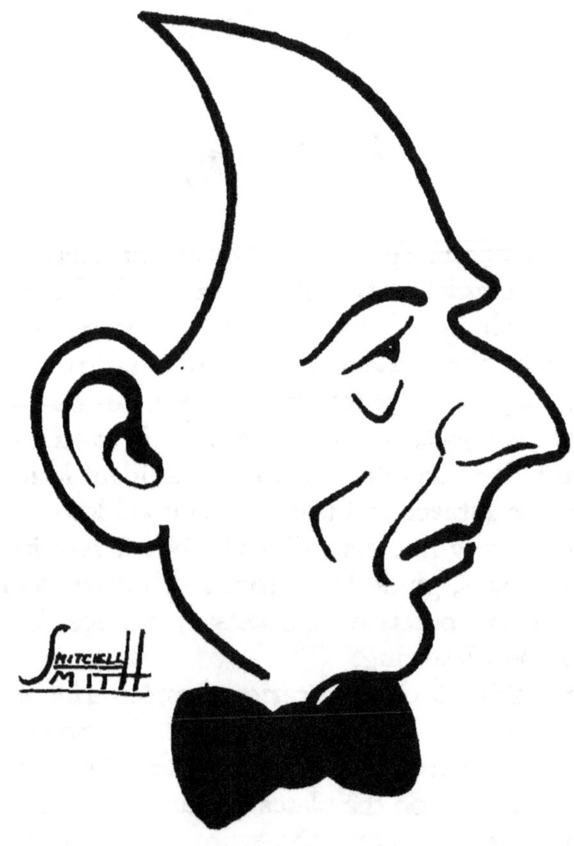

GARRETT

Gothic. All letters having elementary strokes consisting of light and heavy strokes, or rather lines are classified as Roman. Text letters include all styles of Old English, German Text, and the letters derived from the two.

All slanting letters are classified as Italics regardless of their other classifications. Therefore Gothic, Roman, and Text, if drawn slanting are designated as Gothic Italics, Roman Italics, and Text Italics, respectively.

Different styles of lettering pens are adapted to the various classes of alphabets. The pen to use is one that will best produce the elementary strokes of a letter with the least amount of effort. For Gothics there is either a round-nib pen, or a square-nib pen. The chisel pointed pen and the oblong-nib pen are adapted to the Roman and Text letters. However, Romans may be made with a round-nib pen by using double strokes as in the words "DOUBLE-STROKE" on **Plate 19.**

In the words "King" and "Mars" the letters are outlined and shaded. They are Gothics, also, according to the preceding definition. There is quite a variety of lettering on the other plates in this book which the student may study.

For lettering, square the paper with the drawing board and draw horizontal guide lines with a T square as illustrated on **Plate 19.** Note the number and distance of these lines, and how the letters are placed between them. As you will see, the small letters b, d, f, h, j, k, l, and t extend upward from the body of the letters, while the letters g, p, q, and y extend downward. Capitals rest on the line on which the body of the small letters rest, and extend to the uppermost guide line. See "Card" on the plate.

The arrows on the four top lines of lettering illustrate the direction of strokes employed in constructing the letters; and the numerals show the order in which the strokes were made. The beginner should use this plate for a guide, until the strokes and their order have been well learned.

The various strokes overlap in some letters. These complete strokes are illustrated separately on **Plate 19,** for the letters C, d, e, O, Q, S, g, and G.

It is advisable for beginners to draw vertical guide lines, or slanting guide lines for Italics, so that all letters can more easily be made perpendicular, or if Italics, with the same slant.

Lettering should first be drawn in with pencil and then with the proper lettering pen. Special care should be given to the layout of lettering in regard to composition, balance, etc.

Spacing of letters is another important item. There is no fixed rule for the spacing of letters. Some require more space than others, and the combination of letters in some words may determine the space. Some letters of the alphabet are broader than others, while some are narrow. The only practical way to determine the proper space for them is, by one's aesthetic sense; that is, to obtain a pleasing result or effect. Certainly ugly gaps and crowded letters are detrimental to the appearance of lettering.

Lettering provides an outlet for artistic expression, although to a less extent than the fine arts. New letter styles may be originated from the three basic alphabets, and there are many ways of shading them.

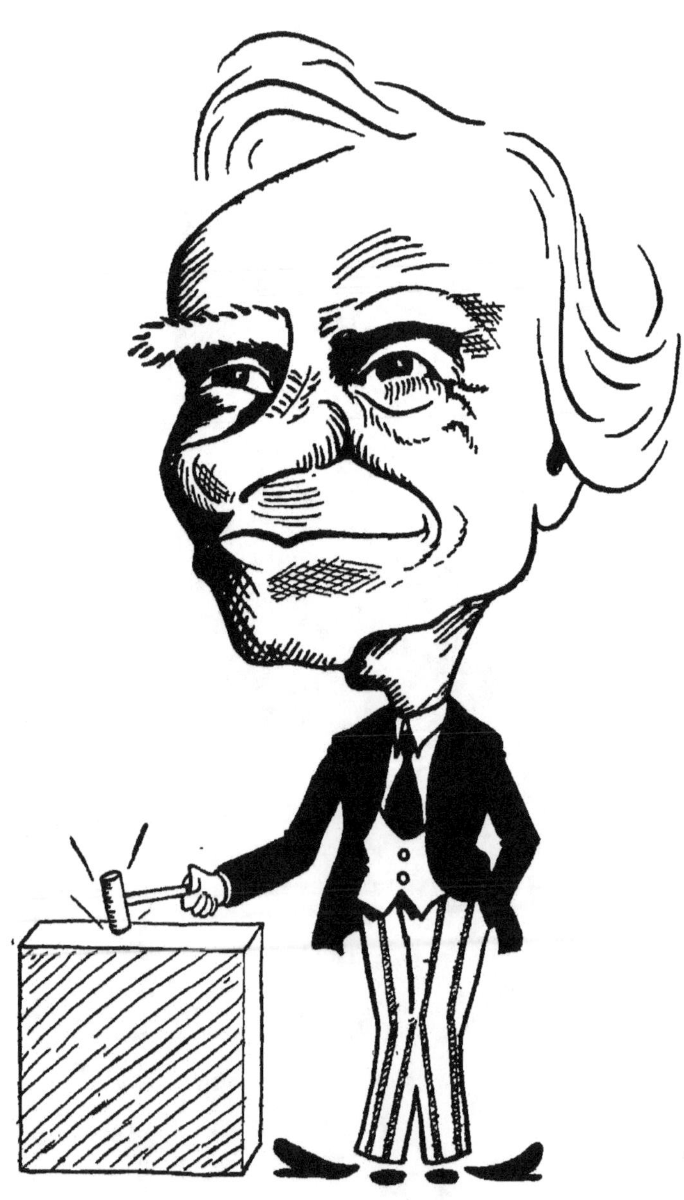

BYRNS

Chapter XI

This and That

Perspective is the art of representing objects, on a plane surface, in three dimensions, as they appear to the observer; the effect of distance on the appearance of objects.

The relative size of an object is determined by the distance it is from the eye. If you look through a small aperture, such as a hole punched in paper with a small pencil lead, you may see a large mountain at a distance. Another good example of perspective is a railroad track. Stand in the center of the track and see how the rails run upward and inward till they meet and vanish at an indefinite point. In perspective, objects of this nature, below the level of the eye, ascend to eye level; above the level of the eye they descend to the eye level. So telegraph wires beside the R. R. would descend and bear inward toward the track until they converge and vanish at eye level, which is also the "Horizon Line."

Besides the relative sizes of objects in perspective, there is another way to obtain the illusion of distance in drawings. This is by color. Color is less brilliant at a distance, than it is nearer the eye. In line drawings, distant objects are simply drawn with finer lines, which really amounts to the same thing.

In art, arranging objects in a pleasing group is called composition. To obtain a pleasing group, there must be a balance of the objects represented, according to size, color, and importance. If there is much bright color near one side of a painting, and subdued colors are used for the remainder of the picture, then the attention of the eye will be attracted by the bright color to that particular side.

Objects of most interest should be placed near the center of the composition. Tones and values should be balanced. No large open or blank spaces should be permitted to detract from a composition. To fill in such places lettering and other detail may be used in cartoons. For compositions representing outdoor scenes, outdoor details may be employed, as: clouds, trees, smoke, automobiles, houses, fences, etc. For indoor detail, pictures on wall, windows and curtains, doors and furniture may be used. On the plates in this book, note how large open spaces were avoided by the placing of the comic figures, lettering and other detail.

As suggested before, you should keep a "morgue of clippings," for reference as models when needed. Of course you will only want to keep unusually good examples of various kinds, techniques, actions, etc.; otherwise you would collect a large number that would very likely never be used. Practically all artists do this, because no one can draw just anything from memory. Clippings are also an aid in getting ideas for drawings. A composition in a clipping may be adapted for an original drawing, in which entirely different objects or figures may be used, according to ones need. Don't copy outright an entire figure or composition, in the same technique, for this is really stealing, or at least, attempting to steal. Stealing another's ideas, either in Art or Literature, is termed Plagiarism and is punishable by Federal Statutes pertaining to Copyrights.

To copyright drawings before submitting them to Editors or Publishers is unnecessary, as well as expensive. Only printed matter, with a few exceptions, may be copyrighted, and then it is necessary to pay a fee. However, if you should publish something you wish to Copyright, write to the Register of Copyrights, Library of Congress, Washington, D. C., requesting the required forms and information. You should do this previous to the printing of the work for there are some requirements as to the printing; especially of the Copyright Notice, which should contain the date of Copyright, and name of the owner of same. There is also a specified place for this notice in books.

Drawings intended for sale should be made on a good grade of Bristol Board, and a margin left all the way around the drawings. They should be mailed flat, and require first class postage. Enclose postage for the return of the drawings. Only send good drawings of a reasonable quantity. Enclose a neat and terse letter to the one you are sending the drawings to, written with pen and ink or typewriter if possible, on plain white letter size paper, 8½ x 11. It is unnecessary to tell the

Editor your qualifications in submitting free lance work, for he will consider it upon its merits regardless of your training and experience. If he likes your work and it is suitable for his publication he will purchase it, otherwise he will return it to you if you have enclosed proper and sufficient postage for that purpose. It is the quality of your work, and not how or why you can do it, that interest editors most.

Caricatures are becoming rather popular, and are widely used in Newspapers, Magazines, Books, and other printed matter. Some of the magazines using caricatures are, **The Saturday Evening Post, American Magazine, Colliers, Bookman, Esquire** and others.

Another good method for selling caricatures is to sell the original caricature to the subject from which it was made. Hobby Caricatures are perhaps best for this purpose. They are made with a large head and a small humorous body, illustrating some hobby or sport; such as: Painting, Fishing, Skiing, Golf, etc.

Caricatures are also employed to a considerable extent in the theatrical business. They are used in Posters, Newspaper Ads., and in Theatrical Displays. An example of the latter is the caricature by Eddie Burgess, see **Frontispiece.**

Always strive for originality. Do much sketching, and try out any idea you should think of. The greatest pleasure in Art should be in creating something original. How exalted and wonderful it is to create something good!

Practice caricaturing from life and from photographs clipped from magazines and newspapers. Good studies may also be found in Histories and English Books containing pictures of writers and poets.

Success is to the ambitious and the persistent. Do not be discouraged if you do not gain recognition immediately; few artists have. There is pleasure in Art for the one that enjoys drawing, regardless of profit or recognition; and one who does not care for drawing will perhaps never succeed anyway. So, my dear reader, if you really like to draw, take SUCCESS as your goal and let nothing whatever deter you from your course. If you do this your success is assured.

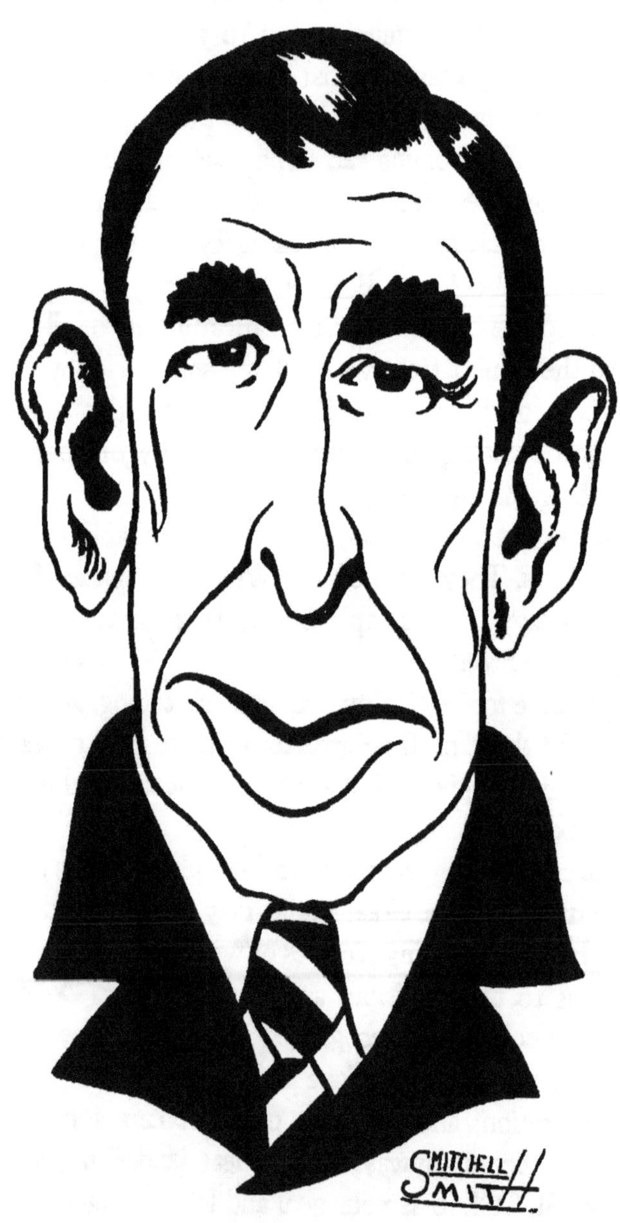

TARKINGTON

Chapter XII

Assignments and Suggestions

This final chapter of assignments is included to facilitate study of the principles of caricaturing explained and illustrated in the preceding chapters. The author knows from personal experience that it is much easier to study when one has definite assignments of work to be done. Although it is presumed that the majority of people who use this book will have had some practice in drawing, many will be beginners, or at most, not far advanced, and it is especially difficult for the novice to study without a guide for his efforts. The amateur needs something of the professional's experience and imagination in the form of suggestions to add to his own initiative in producing an original work of art— both drawings and suggestions which he can grasp and follow. To a great extent the imagination must be developed. However this does not mean that some are not gifted with more imagination than others, but that whatever imaginative powers one has must be developed, just as a very talented artist must develop his talent by study. Even Michael Angelo, one of the greatest artists of all time, had to learn to draw just the same as a less talented artist, but he probably learned much quicker and with less effort.

Perspective is the science of representing things as they appear rather than as they really are. It is accomplished by the careful reproduction of lines, colors, lights and shades. But the most perfect drawing cannot entirely overcome some degree of flatness in a picture. This is due to the fact that an artist draws only one picture and our eyes see two pictures when viewing objects in reality. Look at some cylindrical object such as a barrel with the left eye, closing the right, then vice versa and you will note that you see farther around the right side with the right eye, and farther around the left side with the left eye. So each eye gives a slightly different picture of the barrel or other object. These two visual images are combined in the brain into one visual percept. By means of the stereoscope one looks at two pictures, seeing them as one, and the objects in the picture stand out in startling perspective.

There are four essentials of a good caricature: a likeness of the person portrayed, exaggeration, simplicity or economy of lines used in drawing, and originality. The best method of attaining these four essentials in one drawing is by much study and sketching, trying the different ways of drawing one caricature. A good rule to follow in doing this is to first draw a picture as much like the subject as possible, not exaggerating. Next make another drawing exaggerating the most distinctive characteristics and simplifying the drawing, leaving out lines not necessary. Keep sketching, exaggerating and simplifying as much as the drawing will stand and still retain a good likeness. Add your own originality of execution and you have the most you can do with your present knowledge and skill. Some faces seem to have been made to order for cartoonists while others are very difficult. It is only by experiment that one learns the easy ones. Of course such simplified drawings exaggerating the most distinctive characteristics of the person they portray are little more than suggestions of those prominent features which our eyes catch, our minds suggesting the balance.

ASSIGNMENTS

NUMBER 1

(1) With a Gillott's pen number 303, practice the vertical parallel lines in Figure A, Plate 1. Practice these lines until you can draw them evenly and steadily, free from nervousness. Be careful to space them as evenly as possible. Unless you have done considerable work with a drawing pen, it will be necessary to draw them slowly at first. Speed will come with practice. Your purpose when beginning should be perfection rather than speed.

(2) Figure B on the same plate is also produced with the 303 pen. Only slight pressure is used in such light lines as these. Practice these horizontal strokes. It is practically impossible to draw perfectly straight lines without the aid of a ruler or some kind of straight

edge. Free hand lines are not supposed to be straight hard lines, such as the draftsman employs; but should have slight variation to convey feeling, and variety to prevent monotony.

(3) The wavy vertical lines in Figure C should be less difficult for the beginner than the preceding exercises.

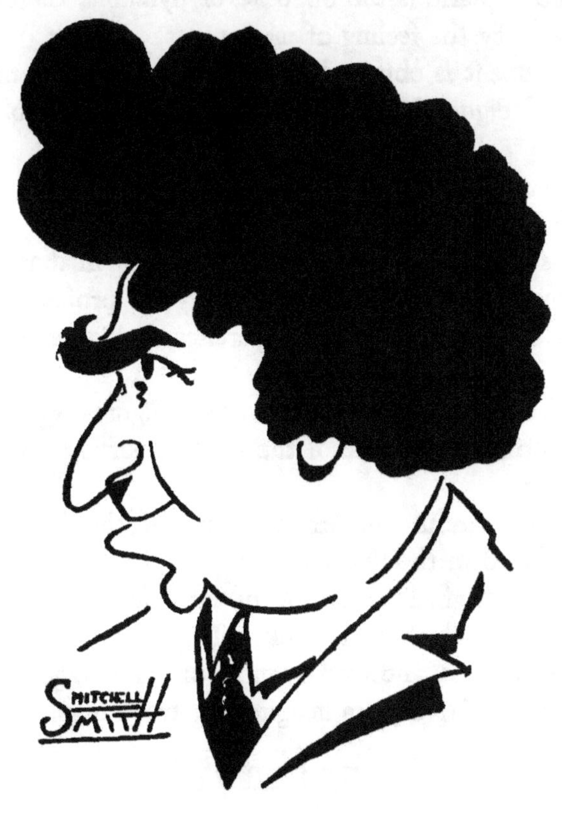

MARTINELLI

(4) Figure D illustrates shaky lines which have movement from left to right. They are termed dynamic because they convey the sense of movement. This movement is obtained by the longer oblique stroke opposed by a shorter stroke, and by the variation. However, the variation or irregularity serves mostly as a relief from the monotony which results from exact repetition of a stroke or motif.

(5) Figures E and F are termed crosshatch. This type of tone is often employed for shadows and not infrequently for shading of clothes. Practice them until you have gained some facility and sureness in handling the pen.

(6) G shows a combination of the lines in Figures C and D to form a dynamic crosshatch. Parallel lines or straight lines in crosshatch are static. **Static** is the opposite of **dynamic**; therefore, static lines do not convey the feeling of motion.

(7) Movement is obtained by opposing strokes in the herringbone weave of Figure H. Practice this pattern of strokes with a larger pen.

(8) Make several copies each of Figures I, J, K, and L. Also of N, O, and P. Spatter work will be treated later.

(9) It is important that you attain facility in drawing graded lines. Without this ability you can hardly do professional looking work. Make several sheets of the exercises in Figures Q, R, S, T, and U.

(10) Also see what you can do with Figures V and W. Remember that originality is one of the most important aspects of any kind of art.

(11) Make careful and exact copies of the four caricatures which are included in the first chapter.

(12) Make original caricatures of these four men. Feel free to make any changes which you think will improve them. You may change the expressions, and employ more or less exaggeration according to your mood. Give your imagination free range.

NUMBER 2

(1) With a ruler or T-square draw the lines as in Figure 1, Plate 2. Draw them twice as large as they appear on this plate, for you remember that drawings are usually reduced to ½ size in reproduction. Figure 1 should be drawn in pencil. Over these pencil guide lines sketch in the face of Figure 2. Finish as in Figure 3, draw it with ink, then erase the pencil guide lines and you have an interesting head.

(2) Copy Figure 4, same plate, and add a small body if you care to.

(3) For further practice in drawing the head in direct front view, copy Figures 2 and 3, Plate 3, and the caricature of Clemenceau on page 27.

(4) Figures 4 and 5, on Plate 3, illustrate the head in 2/3 front view. Draw these.

(5) Draw the caricature of Bolivar, on page 26.

(6) Going back to Plate 2, make ten diagrams of Figure 1. Using these guide lines, draw ten original comic heads, front view. To get variety in your work, vary the features, such as different shaped and sized eyes, noses of different length and shape, etc.

(7) Using similar diagrams, draw ten side view (profile) comic heads. Employ the same form of variation as in exercise 6.

(8) The head in 2/3 front is more difficult than the front or profile. But this greater difficulty should only serve as a greater incentive to conquer, instead of as a discouraging factor. Draw ten heads in 2/3 front. Block them out with the aid of guide lines. If you need further help, refer to drawings in this book and to cartoons in magazines, such as Esquire, Colliers, Saturday Evening Post, etc.

(9) Age. Draw five heads of old men and five of old women. Refer to this subject in Chapter II.

(10) Youth. Draw five heads of children.

NUMBER 3

(1) For the purpose of memorizing the essentials of expression, make several copies of each expression illustrated on Plate 4.

(2) For each expression draw a small comic head but simplify further the features and expression.

(3) Draw each expression in profile and 2/3 front view.

(4) For further practice of expression turn to Plate 5 and make exact copies of Figures 1, 2, and 3. Can you express the smile, the stern and angry expressions?

(5) Figures 4, 5, 6, and 7 show Der Fuehrer smiling, angry, sad, and interested, respectively.

(6) The cartoonist makes animals express their feelings also. This is illustrated by Figures 8 and 9 on the same plate (5). Copy these.

(7) Copy outright the caricature of Foch on page 33. Repro-

duce exactly the parallel line and crosshatch shading in this drawing.

(8) Draw a donkey's head, side view, smiling.

(9) Draw an elephant's head as above, except substitute **anger** for **smile.**

NUMBER 4

(1) Draw about fifty eyes in various shapes, sizes, and degrees of exaggeration ranging from mere dots and slits to the large, "come-hither" eyes of an irresistible young lady.

(2) Draw a large variety of ears in all shapes and sizes.

(3) As for noses—make them long, short, slender, fat, roman, pug, crooked, and flat. Draw them front, profile, and 2/3 front.

(4) Copy Figures 2 and 4 on Plate 6. Also both caricatures of Masefield on this same plate.

(5) Draw several original heads, using for features, suitable ones selected from your work in exercises 1, 2, and 3. Also get variety and exaggeration in hair, jaws, and chins. Make double chins, pointed chins, chins with beard and stubble beard.

(6) Copy the head of Bismarck, page 39. Change any part you wish, but be sure to retain a likeness of the subject.

(7) Copy all three drawings on Plate 8. Note the snorting expression of the pony.

(8) Copy Figures 1 and 3, Plate 7. Note the difference in exaggeration and technique. For an explanation of spatter shading as used in Figure 3, refer to Chapter VII and the accompanying Plate, No. 14.

NUMBER 5

(1) In all exercises for this section, employ the method of block-ing out figures as illustrated in Figures A, B, 1, and 4, Plate 9. Copy Figure 3 following the procedure as illustrated.

(2) Copy Figures 5, 6, and 7. Get the same expressions and actions as in the originals. Also same shading.

(3) Originate 5 comic figures in front view. Get a selection of fat, slender, tall, and short figures.

(4) Same as Exercise 3 except in side view.

(5) Same as 3 and 4 except 2/3 front.

NUMBER 6

(1) Read carefully the chapter on action before beginning the following exercises.

(2) Copy all figures on Plate 10.

(3) Plate 11 illustrates several good action studies. Copy these carefully.

(4) Copy the action and shading illustrations on Plate 12.

(5) For a change and rest from figures, copy the caricatures on pages 44, 49, and 51. Also the one on page 52.

(6) Draw a boxer, side view, punching a bag. Get plenty of action into it.

(7) Draw Hitler making a speech. Make hair dishevelled, eyes wild with emotion, mouth opened wide, and arms and hands wildly gesticulating. Place him on a balcony and very simply, suggest a crowd listening. Remember simplicity is essential for good cartoons. Good cartoons suggest rather than portray faithfully. They only show the essential with everything superfluous omitted.

(8) Draw a football player kicking a football. Can you adequately represent a hard kick?

(9) Draw a baseball player running to first base and really make him step on it! Suggest the stadium full of wildly cheering fans.

(10) Do two action figures of your own choosing.

NUMBER 7

(1) For further practice in the use of parallel lines, crosshatch, and spatter in shading, copy the drawings on pages 56 and 57. But before doing the exercises for this chapter, reread it (Chapter VII) carefully.

(2) Draw a cube of about 2 inches square. Use a model if possible, and have the light coming from only one direction. Shade the block, using tones of different values for the different planes to bring out the form forcefully. Also represent the shadow cast.

(3) Draw a cylinder standing on end, about 4 inches high and 2 inches wide. How can you show the curvature of the surface? It also casts a shadow. Draw the shadow.

(4) A chair is setting in the sunlight. Draw it with a shadow beneath. Use crosshatch for the shadow. Does the shadow seem to lie flat on the ground? Does it stand on edge? Why?

(5) A burglar is running very rapidly beside a board fence. The moonlight casts a shadow from his feet to the fence and a part of his shadow is on the fence. Draw him. Suggest houses on other side of fence, also a few bushes and trash to represent an alley scene. Have you gotten a pleasing contrast between your light and dark tones?

(6) Draw a fat man in a boat fishing. The boat is small and the man is so heavy that it is almost standing on end. Draw shadow beneath the end of boat which is above water. Also the shadow of the man is shown on the water. Can you represent water simply? This is a good exercise.

(7) Draw a man's coat, front view, without the man. Place shadows under lapels and buttons. Make wrinkles as if coat were on a man.

(8) Draw a vest and trousers as if they were on a man but don't draw the man. Place shadows where needed.

(9) A pair of shoes are on the floor. The toes are turned up slightly. Draw them with shadows which emphasize this and show contact with the floor.

(10) Remember all these tricks of shading and shadows. Draw an original composition, and shade it according to what you have learned.

NUMBER 8

(1) Copy the caricature of Jack Dempsey on page 63. Reproduce the technique of the original drawing.

(2) Copy the drawing on page 62. Note this is entirely different from the one on page 63.

(3) Copy the composition on page 64. This drawing has cross-hatch, parallel lines, and heavy stripes. The solid black affords contrast and lends color to the drawing. Note the flying notes which signify that Paderewski is playing.

(4) Copy the drawing of Coffin on page 44. All drawings should be made twice the size which they appear in this book. Note the simplicity of this drawing. Can you obtain the same expression as the author has depicted?

(5) In the two caricatures of Pershing, Plate 13, page 54, note

the difference in treatment or technique. Copy these as exercises in technique. Also make a drawing of Sam Insull.

(6) Copy the two caricatures of Howard Thurston, Plate 15. Note the simplification and exaggeration in Figure 2.

(7) Using any model you prefer, draw a caricature using soft lead pencil and wash.

(8) Draw another one with crayon or any other medium you prefer. Learn to exercise initiative and originality. If you have an air brush try a caricature in this medium.

NUMBER 9

(1) After rereading Chapter IX, make copies of all animals on Plates 17 and 18. Do not draw them just to get them done, for such work will not be of any help in developing your ability to draw. Draw them carefully with the same actions and expressions, unless you think you can improve them.

(2) Draw a donkey, side view, with Jack Garner in the saddle. Suggest a landscape of cactus and distant mesas. Can you make the donkey look lazy and slow? How should his ears be? His head? What about shading and shadows?

(3) With the help of Plate 8, draw a bucking horse ridden by a cowpuncher. Have him holding a ten gallon hat in one hand, the reins with the other.

(4) Draw a woodpecker pecking on a snag. How can you suggest flying dust and the rapidity of his head movements?

(5) Draw the Russian bear eating a man which is labeled Finland. Draw this in the style of a propaganda cartoon for newspapers.

(6) Draw the British lion being subdued by Mahatma Gandhi. This is another propagandistic idea. How can you best express the idea?

(7) Draw an elephant, labeled G.O.P., standing on rear feet, boxing gloves on front feet, punching a bag which is labeled New Deal.

(8) Take a good gag pertaining to a man and his wife and apply it to a rooster and hen; then draw an illustration of the joke.

(9) Draw Peter Rabbit riding on a sled which is being pulled by a dog. Make a drawing of this idea which will interest children.

(10) Draw any five animals you wish with any actions and expressions, and in any views you choose. But have expressions consistent with action and vice versa. Develop your imagination by originating ideas. Develop originality by drawing correctly but differently.

NUMBER 10

(1) Copy the lettering on Plate 19. Draw pencil guide lines first and lay out the lettering in pencil also, before beginning with the lettering pen. It is not necessary to make the fine arrowed lines which are on the plate merely for the purpose of indicating the direction and order of the stroke.

(2) Copy the words "Drawing the Head" as they appear on Plate 2, page 22. Note the shadows cast by letters upon other letters.

(3) From Plate 3, page 24, copy the word "William II." This is a style often used in newspaper cartoons. Letter the following words in the same style: "Crown Prince," "John Dewey," "Ferdinand."

(4) The word "Coontz," page 32, shows another style appropriate for cartoons. In the same style letter "Marshal Foch."

(5) Letter the words "Brandenburg" and "Hohenzollern" in the style of the word "Hindenburg" on page 38.

(6) Letter your name with conjoined letters as in "Ignace Paderewski," page 64. Letter the word Roosevelt in the same style. Draw the two o's interlocking or passing through each other as two links of a chain.

(7) Letter several other words in a style similar to that of the above exercise, but shade the letters differently. Always use guide lines.

NUMBER 11

(1) Draw a house in perspective, comic style. Have sunlight falling from right to left and shade accordingly. Where will the shadows fall?

(2) Draw a straight road viewed from its middle. On either side is a fence. There is also a telephone line on one side of the road. All lines will converge at the horizon.

(3) Draw a table in perspective. Also the interior of a room showing windows and door in perspective. For help in these per-

spective drawings refer to Chapter XI. Remember that distance is suggested by graduated tones, the darkest in foreground and lightest in the distance.

(4) For an exercise in composition, draw an interior scene showing a man and a pretty girl, furniture, windows, pictures on walls, etc. Arrange various items of the picture to put across the idea, for balance of objects, balance of tones with most important items most noticeable, those of less importance subdued, and those which are superfluous, entirely eliminated.

NUMBER 12

(1) In magazines, histories, encyclopedias, etc., look up pictures of the following people and draw caricatures of them, applying what you have learned in the eleven preceding sections: William Bankhead, Leopold Stokowski, Al Smith, Jack Garner, John W. Davis, Adolph S. Ochs, Bernard M. Baruch, Dr. Raymond Ditmars, W. H. Woodin, Senator Borah, Dr. Raymond Moley, Sen. Pat Harrison, "Dizzy" Dean, Bill Tilden, Clark Gable, Joe E. Brown, Jimmy Durante, Ernest Lubitsch, William G. McAdoo, Charles G. Dawes, Calvin Coolidge, Jim Farley, Herbert Hoover, J. Edgar Hoover, Eugene O'Neil, and F. D. Roosevelt.

Note: The Author of this book offers profitable and constructive criticism of your work. Address him, care of the Publisher.

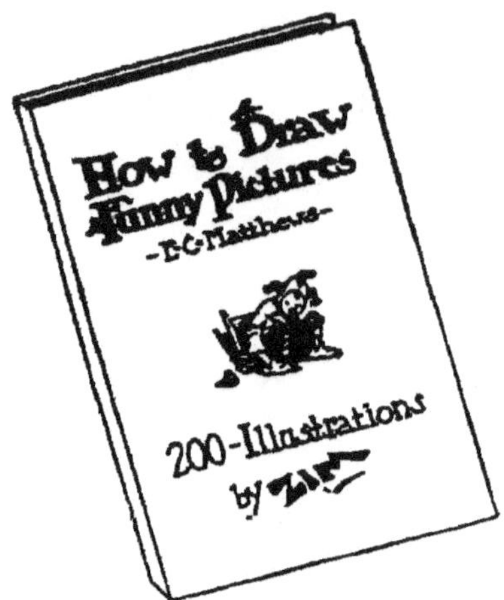

A COMPLETE COURSE IN

CARTOONING

Size 6½ x 10¼ inches.

160 Pages, printed on Plate Paper.

Cloth Binding $2.00

CONTAINS over two hundred original drawings from the pen, pencil and brush of Eugene Zimmerman (Zim), whose work needs no introduction.

Every imaginable phase of cartooning is explained and illustrated in full.

Teachers, preachers and professional chalk-talkers will find the book full of material that can be worked into illustrated lectures. Authors and humorists may illustrate their own writing. Commercial artists, ad writers and sign painters will find a wealth of humorous suggestions that can be applied profitably.

School and college students can turn their art ambitions into profitable channels, and even the professional cartoonist will find this a reference book worth many times its price.

BEGINNING with the simplest kind of practice sketches, the book leads you through a dozen interesting chapters to complete mastery of humorous illustrating. Not a dull page in the course.

Table of Contents by Chapters.

Introduction.
A Word about Materials.
Practice Sketches—Faces in Caricature.
Comic Figures and Simple Cartoons.
Wash Drawing.
Action and Perspective.
Cartoon Animals and Backgrounds.
Character and Expression.
Seasonal and Holiday Cartoons.
School and College Humor.
Illustrated Jokes and How to Sell Them.
Picture Animating and Chalk Talking.
Humorous Articles—How to·Illustrate Them.
Sports Cartooning.
Political and Editorial Cartooning.

Write for our complete free catalog of books on Lettering, Sign and Scene Painting, Show Card Writing, Furniture Finishing, Mixing Colors, Painting and Decorating, Interior Decoration, Designing, etc.

FREDERICK J. DRAKE & CO.

PUBLISHERS
600-610 W. Van Buren St.
CHICAGO, U. S. A.

The Art of
CARICATURING

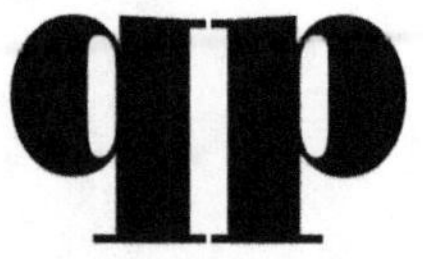

Visit us at *www.quidprobooks.com*.